OPE

Panama

by Bruce Morris

Open Road Travel Guides – designed for the amount of time you *really* have for your trip!

Open Road Publishing

Open Road's new travel guides.
Designed to cut to the chase.
You don't need a huge travel encyclopedia – you need a *selective guide* to steer you right. If you're going on vacation for a few weeks or less, get a guide that brings you the *best* of any destination for the amount of time you *really* have for your trip!

Open Road – the guide you need for the trip you want.

The New Open Road *Best Of* Travel Guides.
Right to the point.
Uncluttered.
Easy.

Open Road Publishing
www.openroadguides.com

ISBN 10: 1-59360-168-9
ISBN 13: 978-1-59360-168-3
Library of Congress Control No. 2012947558

About the Author

Bruce Morris lives on Lake Atitlan in Guatemala He is a travel writer and owns restaurant Club Ven Acá. He is also the author of *Open Road's Best of the Florida Keys & Everglades, Open Road's Best of Guatemala,* and with his brother Charlie Morris, writes *Open Road's Best of Costa Rica.* Visit www.brucemorris.com to learn more about Bruce and view his photos from around the world.

For photo credits and acknowledgments, turn to page 199.

CONTENTS

Your Passport to the Perfect Trip!

Maps

Open Road's Best Of
PANAMA

1. INTRODUCTION

Panama packs a lot of punch in a small country. There are numerous attractions, and good transportation infrastructure. **Ecotourism is just beginning.** Almost half of Panama is still forested, with about a quarter of these forests preserved in government or privately operated preserves. UNESCO has named **Darien** a Natural World Heritage Site and a World Biosphere Reserve. Their primary forest is the largest in Central America. Birders and ecotourists flock to immerse themselves in one of the most species-rich and biodiverse regions on the planet.

Both the Caribbean and Pacific coasts are lined with **dramatic white-sand beaches** and picture postcard-perfect tropical islands. If you like lots of action, throbbing music and exotic umbrella drinks with your beach, you can find it. If you want a tropical island with white sand and coconut palms all to yourself, you can find that, too.

Panama is a sleeper tourism destination. As travel to Central America grows, travel to Panama is starting to boom. I dislike trite clichés, but here goes: Panama is the new Costa Rica. I also prefer not to compare the two countries—I love them both. But the things that attract the growing tourist hordes to Costa Rica are all present in Panama, in profusion and with far less tourist traffic.

Come find out for yourself!

2. OVERVIEW

Panamanians are friendly and outgoing. They are tourist- and gringo-friendly. The average Panamanian has a good impression of Americans and is curious about visitors. Although there is poverty, there is a large and growing prosperous middle class. **Street crime is rare.** Panama City and the other parts of Panama are as safe as most of North America or Europe.

Panama is about the size of a stretched-out South Carolina, or roughly three times the size of Wales. I have trouble classifying it as a third world country since, for the most part, Panama enjoys a **first-world infrastructure.** It's a modern country with good roads, telecommunications and world-class banking and business services. There are airports scattered around most of the country. This of course, excludes Darien, and vast areas of the highlands, which remain, for the most part, free of electricity. The rainforest stretches unbroken for many miles of swamp and jungle.

Convenient for the currency-befuddled, **Panama uses US dollars.** This also makes it an economical destination during the dollar's current scuba dive on world financial markets. Prices are generally about the same as in the US or slightly cheaper—roughly half the level of prices in Europe.

Flights from the US are cheap. It's **only a four-hour flight** from Atlanta—closer than many Caribbean destinations.

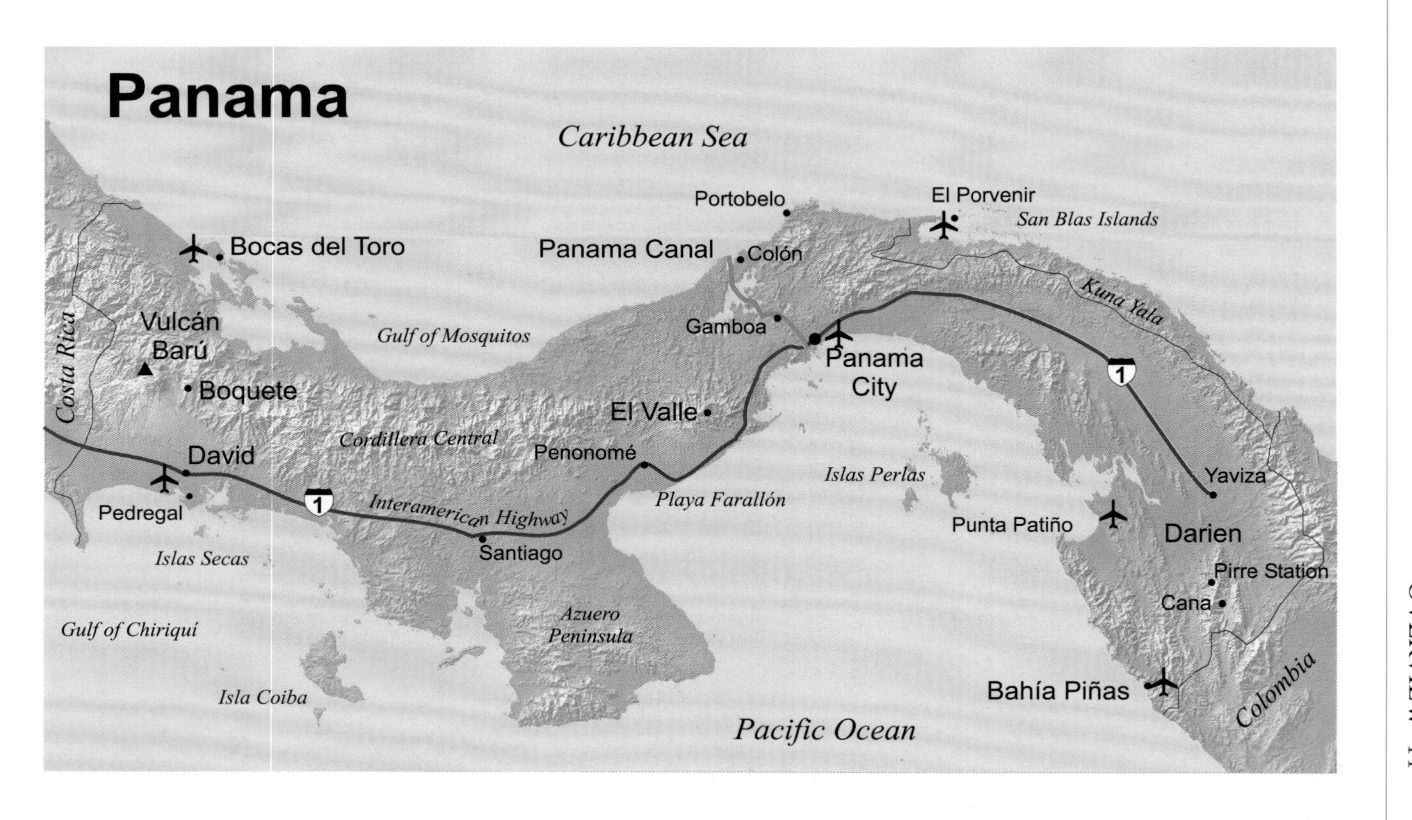
Panama
Caribbean Sea
Portobelo
El Porvenir
San Blas Islands
Bocas del Toro
Panama Canal
Colón
Kuna Yala
Vulcán
Barú
Gulf of Mosquitos
Gamboa
Panama
City
Boquete
El Valle
1
Costa Rica
Cordillera Central
David
Penonomé
Islas Perlas
Yaviza
Pedregal
1
Interamerican Highway
Playa Farallón
Punta Patiño
Darien
Santiago
Islas Secas
Pirre Station
Cana
Azuero
Peninsula
Gulf of Chiriquí
Isla Coiba
Bahía Piñas
Colombia
Pacific Ocean

With both the Caribbean and Pacific coasts to choose from, **fishing, diving and kayaking** are excellent. More angling world records have been set in Panama than in any other country on the planet. Add whitewater rafting in the mountains.

The climate is great. Trade winds tend to keep things cool and there are no hurricanes or major earthquakes.

The **great food** in Panama is reason enough to come by itself. Fresh seafood is standard fare. Fresh vegetables, tropical fruits and other local ingredients are used to create a unique Panamanian cuisine—a fusion (love that word) of the different cultures that make up Panama: Spain, indigenous, Caribbean, African, Asian.

Funky **surf camps and high-end luxury resorts** cater to young backpackers, Rolling Stones level celebrities and everyone in between. Modern high-rise business hotels in Panama City compete by adding another heliport. Several of the world's best ecolodges are found in Panama.

Panama City

For the historically-minded, Panama's capital city offers **Casco Viejo**, the old, historic part of town, an architecturally interesting **World Heritage Site** experiencing a well-thought-out restoration. Throughout the city there are quaint B&Bs, boutique hotels and big city business hotels with helicopter landing pads and five star services.

Yet Panama City is a **modern and cool town**. It's a financial boomtown with amazingly tall and skinny skyscrapers all over the place and hundreds more going up by the minute. The dramatic skyline rivals Hong Kong. Completely unlike most Latin American capitals, Panama City (simply called

Panamá by the locals) is modern, relatively clean, relatively safe and interesting. The magnificent skyline is dotted with hundreds of construction cranes as luxury high-rise condominiums, banks and office towers rise all over the city like mushrooms after a rainstorm. The throbbing, hot nightlife is legendary. There are dozens of wonderful restaurants.

More or less in the center of the country, it's a good base for exploring the country and a worthy destination in itself.

The Panama Canal

This feat of engineering triumph fascinates the mechanically or historically minded. My wife tells me it's a guy thing. I'm not so sure. **Huge Panamax freighters**, designed to be as big as can possibly fit in the locks, cruise ships and oil tankers pass within arm's reach. The three enormous lock systems are entrancing as they raise and lower the huge ships.

The wonderful new **Miraflores Lock Visitor Center** has exhibits, films and a restaurant overlooking the lock's operations. Not to be missed! **Gatún Lake**, which was formed by damming up **Rió Chagres**, is chock full of peacock bass and crocodiles, and is surrounded by tropical rainforests loaded with monkeys, sloths and birds. On Saturdays, you can book trips through the locks or complete transits of the canal. A partial transit of the canal should be part of every visitor's itinerary. A major, multi-billion dollar widening of the canal is now underway.

Bocas del Toro

Perhaps the most popular area for tourists in Panama, Bocas is a group of small islands scattered around the shallows in the stunning, **blue-green Caribbean Sea**. The setting is amazingly tranquil. On the contrary, Bocas Town is a **festering, rowdy party** place appealing to

Panamá

Once you are in the country of Panama, Panama City is simply referred to as *Panamá*, dropping the "City" part. All over the country people say things like: "I talked to my friend in Panamá yesterday" or "I'm going to Panamá next week."

world-traveling youth looking for fun in the sun, surfing, late nights in tropical bars with booming music and **girls gone wild**. The town is very good at this. **Waterside fish restaurants** sit cheek by jowl with tropical bars. Old **gringos going to seed** mingle with dread locked youths studying how it is done.

At night, around the whole town, a loud, booming drone issues from seemingly hundreds of eight-foot high speaker stacks **blasting out music until dawn** or even later. Attempts by some local residents to enforce a curfew on loud music after 3am have failed hopelessly. I love the place.

San Blas Archipelago

As a travel writer, part of my job is coming up with ways to describe **the most beautiful beaches and tropical islands in the world**. Seen one, seen 'em all? No way. Clear water, white sand beaches, and coconut palms waving in the warm tropical breeze—I cannot find the superlatives to properly describe the charms of this idyllic tropical archipelago. The photogenic islands are inhabited by the equally photogenic and fascinating San Blas **Kuna Indians**. These people have rejected most of modern society's "improvements" and are famous for creating reverse appliqué fabrics called *molas*. A visit to one of their villages should be on any visitor's "must do" list.

Gulf of Chiriquí

The huge, mostly pristine Gulf is an important base for thousands of **whales**. Humpback, sperm, blue and killer whales blow, breach, stick their tails up in the air and generally frolic around like porpoises. The **Parque Nacional Coiba** around Isla Coiba has hundreds of superb dive sites and the **marlin fishing** at Montuoso and the Hannibal Bank is legendary. The remote, Robinson Crusoe-like **Islas Secas** are a tropical paradise surrounding one of the planet's most luxurious, remote lodges.

The Central Highlands—Boquete & El Valle

Featuring some of the best **mountain grown coffee** anywhere in the world, the beauty of Boquete and nearby El Valle has attracted an upscale crowd of retired gringos and well-heeled Latinos from all over the world. The beautiful mountain valleys and nearby **cloud forests** are home to an amazing variety of wildlife. Flocks of birders make pilgrimages to the area for glimpses of **resplendent quetzals.** Luxury B&Bs and fine dining await the visitor after days spent exploring the tropical forests in the area.

Darien

The name "Darien" brings to mind mile after mile of endless jungle-clad mountains followed by miles of **jungle covered swamps.** This is serious National Geographic country. There is no "there" there. The whole region has only a couple of very remote jungle camps visitors can get to by small plane and canoe.

The Pacific coast of the province features huge surf, bashing against steep jungle mountainsides so primordial it is hard to imagine any human has ever set foot on some of the peaks. **Fishing for marlin and sailfish** at the world-famous and luxurious Tropic Star Lodge on the Pacific coast is simply the best in the world.

Nightlife & Entertainment

Fine restaurants, casinos, nightclubs of all hues and a few old favorites like Hooters and Hard Rock keep Panama City hopping well past dawn. It is definitely a party and late night kind of place. Music and dance venues explore numerous varieties of the latest hot Latin sounds from reggaeton to Puerto Rican salsa. As Latin American capitals go, Panama City is relatively safe and modern.

The dollar is the deal and buys a level of **extreme late night revelry** hard to match anywhere else, if you know what I mean. Bocas Town has a laid back, twenty-something Caribbean feel with many bars not even opening up much before midnight. The whole town heaves with bass, all night, every night. Panamanians celebrate **Carnival** like no one else.

Food & Drink

A couple of the best Panama City fine dining establishments compare with the fanciest and tastiest of any trendy big city restaurant. Innovative chefs are creating fusions of local tropical ingredients with influences ranging from Old Spain to Japan and China. Locally caught **corvina** served with **patacones** and drizzled with interesting sauces is *muy trendoso* and delicious.

Panamanians take **ceviche** to previously unheard of levels. Street side *cevicherías* serve paper cones filled with chilled ceviche to passersby. This is serious ceviche country.

Típico, or local Panamanian food is savory and interesting; based on local seafood, vegetables, seafood, meat and seafood. **Snapper** and **tuna** are usually fresh and good choices. Large and small shrimp and spiny lobsters are prominent on most menus.

Diving & Snorkeling

What the Pacific lacks in fancy coral and visibility, it makes up for with a thick soup of sea life. The ocean seems to boil with fishy activity. Underwater seamounts meet deep currents bringing exotic **manta rays**, **whales**, **ocean sharks** and pelagics like **marlin** and **sailfish** in close for divers to observe and hang around with. The clear and shallow Caribbean water offers divers and snorkelers **coral gardens** and hours of underwater fun. The country has several underwater protected areas offering good diving and snorkeling.

Surfing

Legendary breaks like **Morro Negrito**, **Punta Brava** and **Dumpers** attract the most adventurous, extreme surfers. Dependable waves and funky beach party towns make Panama a top destination for surfers of all skill levels. **Funky surf camps** offer visitors a comfortable way to get into the local scene without a luxury budget.

Fishing

Few places in the world offer the level of angling found on Panama's Pacific coast. More **world records** have been set in Panama than in any other part of the world, by far. From giant billfish to delicious snapper, tuna and dorado, Panama is, perhaps, the very best place on the planet to pursue game fish. **Luxury lodges** and **funky fishing camps** lure anglers from all over the world.

Bird Watching

With **more than 900 species** identified, Panama is one of the top bird watching destinations on the planet. Birders will find they add significantly to their life list in just their first few hours in the country. Hardcore twitchers walk out of the airport upon their arrival and start birding immediately in the parking lot. They walk off and leave their bags going around and around on the luggage carousel to be picked up later.

Some of the world's top birding guides work here. They know the habitat and habits of each particular species, and are equipped with the latest devices to help their guests see the birds they seek: belt mounted iPods loaded with recordings of bird calls to lure in **LBBs** (Little Brown Birds); laser pointers to help aging gringo eyes to spot birds far

Lowland Panama and the area around the canal have about 1/3 of the over 900 bird species found in Panama. This is the most popular birding area in the country. Ant swarms attract ocellated, bicolored and spotted antbirds; frugiforous birds such as **toucans**, red-capped and blue-crowned manakins swirl about.

Pipeline and **Achiote Roads** and the area around the **Metropolitan Nature Park** promise views of rosy thrush-tanagers and lance-tailed manakins. El Valle de Antón (lots of cloud forest) has a variety of **foothill species** such as tody motmot, dull-mantled antbird, sunbittern, orange-bellied trogon.

In Western Panama you'll find **resplendent quetzals**, three-wattled bellbirds, dusky nightjars and two **endemic hummingbirds**. Others native to this area are the fiery-billed araçari, prong-billed barbet and golden-brown chlorophonia. Nothing matches the excitement of encountering an unmanageable, mixed-species flock with countless birds vying for your attention—it may include a rufous-brown tyrannulet.

The central highlands area, Boquete and El Valle, is Panama's second most popular birding area. It is the most likely place to spot the **resplendent quetzal** and **three-wattled bellbirds**.

Bocas del Toro, like the rest of Panama, is loaded with birds but birding is not as well developed there as it is in other parts of the country. The area is home to the endemic Escudo hummingbird as well as white-crowned pigeons, the great tinamou, squirrel cuckoo, and of course the wonderful **Montezuma oropendola**.

Darien has the **harpy eagle**—the king of the jungle. The only species higher on the food chain would be the great cats. Even monkeys fear the harpy. Endemic species include the beautiful treerunner and pirre warbler. Some eastern Darien specials include rufous-cheeked hummingbird, dusky-backed jacamar and varied solitaire. Eastern Panamanian endemics also include the striped-cheeked woodpecker and violet-throated toucanet.

Also in Darien, Cana hosts viridian dacnis, barred puffbird, vinerous and one-colored becards. On the upper slopes, you'll find the toothed-billed hummingbird, ochre-breasted antpitta and choco tapaculo.

Beaches, Parks & Ecolodges

What flavor do you want your beach to come in? **Name a sand color** and there's a beach for you. Panama has spectacular beaches so remote that no one has put a footprint on their sand in years, as well as other beaches teeming with families and young folks of both sexes strutting their stuff.

Top ecotourism destinations like **Darien, El Valle** and the park around **Volcán Barú** offer everything from intense bird guides to zip lines for screaming fun.

Ecolodges like **Canopy Tower** and **Punta Patiño** place you right in the middle of primary tropical forest, yet provide levels of luxury comparable to upscale resorts anywhere. Visitors pursue sightings of tapirs, crocodiles, monkeys and scarlet macaws.

3. PANAMA CITY

Panama City is a very modern, skyscraper-studded, banking and port city full of nightlife and excitement. It is bustling yet laid back. Slick business types zip around in helicopters; loaded fashionistas choke the casinos and nightclubs. Construction cranes pepper the famous, imposing skyline. This is the Latin American Hong Kong. Seemingly hundreds of high-rise towers are under construction, with old ones being torn down to make space for the new ones.

Away from the glow of neon and flow of narco and tourist dollars, the city has the third world mess you would expect in any huge Latin American city. Grit, grime and poverty are an inescapable part of the landscape but, for the most part, Panama City is reasonably clean with functioning infrastructure superior to almost any other Latin American capital. There's a lot to do and see here, and there are many fine tropical attractions nearby.

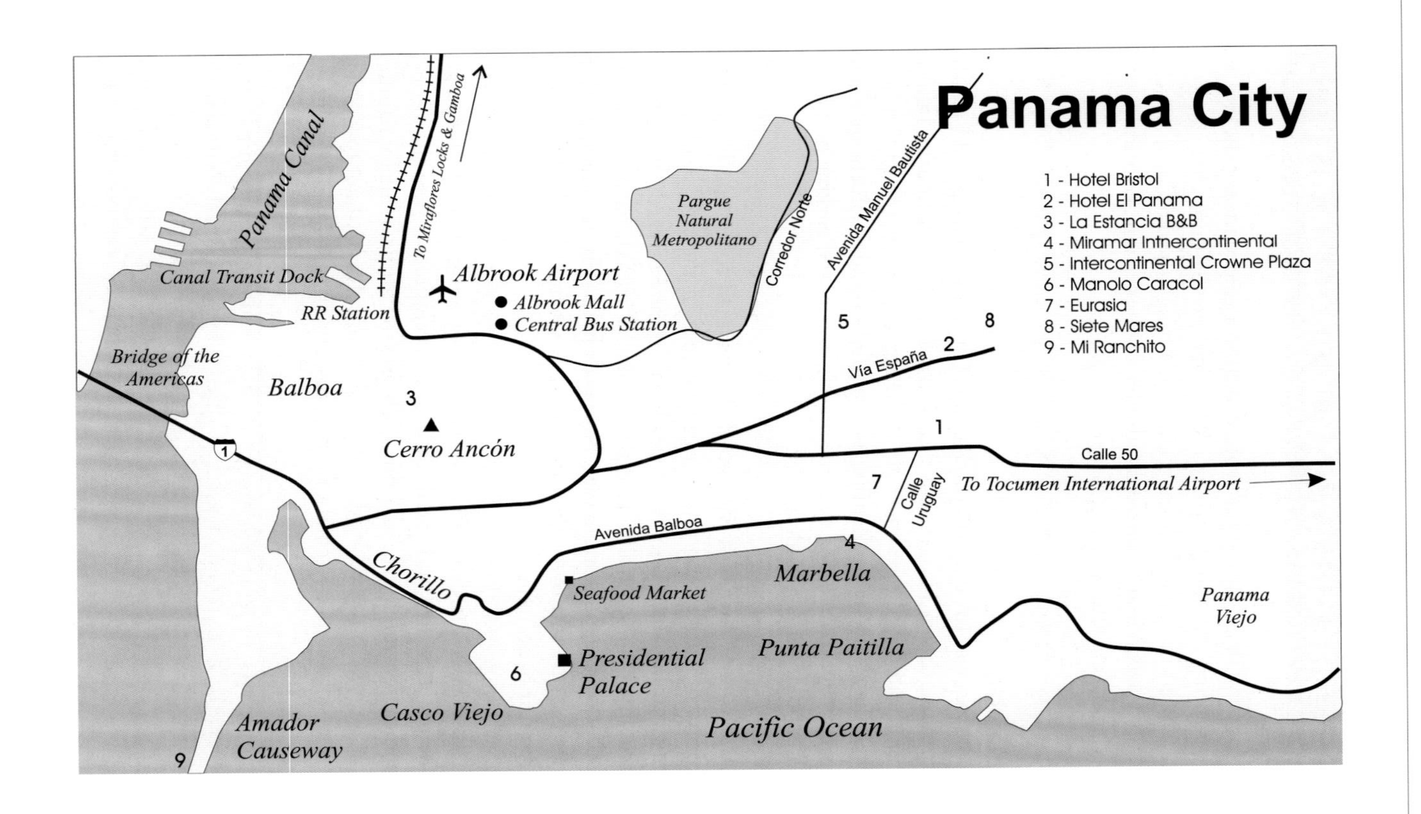
Panama City
1 - Hotel Bristol
2 - Hotel El Panama
3 - La Estancia B&B
4 - Miramar Intnercontinental
5 - Intercontinental Crowne Plaza
6 - Manolo Caracol
7 - Eurasia
8 - Siete Mares
9 - Mi Ranchito
Panama Canal
To Miraflores Locks & Gamboa
Pargue Natural Metropolitano
Corredor Norte
Avenida Manuel Bautista
Canal Transit Dock
Albrook Airport
Albrook Mall
Central Bus Station
RR Station
Bridge of the Americas
Balboa
Vía España
Cerro Ancón
Calle 50
Calle Uruguay
To Tocumen International Airport
Avenida Balboa
Chorillo
Marbella
Seafood Market
Panama Viejo
Presidential Palace
Punta Paitilla
Amador Causeway
Casco Viejo
Pacific Ocean

ONE GREAT DAY IN PANAMA CITY

Spend the morning with your driver on a guided tour of the city, visiting crumbling Panama Viejo and needle-thin, chic condo towers in snooty Paitilla, then drive through the old Canal Zone to Casco Viejo for an elegant dinner. In the evening, go drinking, gambling and whoring or worse.

Morning

The best way to enjoy a day in Panama City is to hire a car and English-speaking driver. This is relatively cheap at $10 to $12 an hour and allows the flexibility to see almost all of the sights in only one day without wearing yourself out. Renting a car would not be much cheaper, and you would have to deal with the big-city traffic and parking problems. A good driver is a guide as well.

After a hotel breakfast with good Panamanian coffee and local fruit, meet your driver and go on a general tour of the city, heading first towards **Panama Viejo**. After viewing the pirate-ravaged ruins (there's not much to see really, just a few piles of rocks), swing briefly by notorious deposed strongman **Noriega**'s house. Even though he is in custody, he still owns the now-run-down house. It'll be fun to talk about it back home.

This part of the drive will give you an opportunity to see the huge, luxurious, walled and gated real estate developments near the airport and the astounding, needle-thin high rises in **Paitilla**. Look for nannies pushing well-frocked kiddies in stylish prams. It's hard not to wonder where all the money comes from to pay for all these luxury dwellings.

ALTERNATE PLAN
Take a half-day tour of the Panama Canal or go fishing for peacock bass on nearby Lake Gatún.

Your driver should take you by the **Papal Nunciatura** where Noriega hid out from the US Army while they blasted Iron Butterfly music at him at extreme volume.

Street Crime?

I'm not really a city person but I love Panama City. It's about as safe as most US cities, which means be careful and take taxis at night. I have no problem with that.

This tactic eventually secured his surrender.

Lunch options include **Mi Ranchito**, a sort of touristy place on the Amador Causeway with *típico* food, or gorging on steak or seafood at **Gaucho's** in the Calle Uruguay neighborhood. Be sure to eat ceviche every time you see it. See Chapter 11, *Best Sleeps & Eats,* for more details on these and other restaurants.

Afternoon

Shop for *molas* (traditional costumes of Kuna women) at **Flory Saltzman's** shop in front of the Hotel El Panama. She has the best deals in the country and a vast selection. If you're hard-core, walk through the **seafood market** near Casco Viejo for a view of what's living in the nearby waters you'll soon be swimming in.

Right next to the seafood market, through one of the worst neighborhoods in town (take a cab), is World Heritage Site **Casco Viejo**. It's like old Havana but with a few trendy shops, restaurants and evening hot spots. After exploring the old walls and picturesque old town, drive through the old Canal Zone on a trip to the overlook for pictures of the canal and the Panama City skyline at **Cerro Ancon**. Take a quick side trip into Balboa in the old Canal Zone to shop at the **Centro de Artesanías Internacional**, located by the YMCA, to buy a couple of **Panama hats** for your pals back home. Don't wear yours until you get to the Atlanta airport.

American Chow

Gringos won't miss the familiar, low culture crap from home they probably would like to escape: Hooters, Hard Rock Café, TGI Friday's, McDonalds and all your old favorites. Too bad, but that's what big cities around the world are like today.

If you have time, you might get your driver to swing you by **Miraflores Locks Visitor Center** for a quick look. It's about 15 minutes out of town if the traffic is not too bad, and is well worth a look if you have an interest in the canal and would like to see huge container ships up close.

Before heading back to your hotel to dress for the evening, when the city lights are just starting to twinkle, manage a swing out on the **Amador Causeway** to see the Panama City skyline and scope out the restaurant and nightlife scene for later.

Evening

Smart casual is the way to go. A night on the town in Panama City can start with drinks at 6pm and end up with more drinks and dancing at 8—that's am, not pm. The action can go on until waaay past dawn at some of the more uninhibited clubs.

Nice restaurants are usually open at 6pm and start to fill up at 8 or 9pm. I suggest dinner at the elegant and wonderful **Eurasia** followed by bar hopping in Calle Uruguay. Include **Il Boccalino** and **Unplugged**. Then, perhaps, a stop by the **Veneto** to check out one of the glitzier (and wilder) casinos in town.

For music lovers, **Havana Rumba** in Casco Viejo is a good place to see locals enjoying contemporary interpretations of Latin classics by local musicians and a few touring greats. This is a serious music listening venue—not a place to carry on loud conversations.

See Chapter 11, *Best Sleeps & Eats,* and Chapter 12, *Best Activities,* for more details on these restaurants and nightlife choices.

A FANTASTIC PANAMA CITY WEEKEND

Full of history, Panama City is a modern, pleasant city bursting with things to do. Good hotels, great restaurants and a heaving nightlife make it a wonderful destination for enjoying urban delights. You can do a lot in a weekend here.

Friday Evening

Settle into the wonderful **Intercontinental Miramar** hotel, have a drink at the pleasant bar enjoying the view out over the Pacific and get ready for dinner at quirky **Manolo Caracol**. It's a tapas-style restaurant right in the middle of the interesting and quaint **Casco Viejo** neighborhood. After dinner, walk a short distance to **La Casona de Las Brujas** to dance to the sounds of US-style rock. Or, also nearby, **La Platea** is *the* spot for jazz and salsa. Cab back to the hotel, crawl through the lobby into the elevator and into your room and to bed.

Saturday

Enjoy your hotel's buffet breakfast of Panamanian coffee, pastries, eggs, *chorizo* and tropical fruit. Get a ride around town to see the sights. Either hire a car and English-speaking driver in advance, or just take taxis from place to place. Taxis are quite inexpensive, but an English-speaking driver can serve as a guide as well and simplify traffic and parking problems.

Start your tour by heading through town roughly towards the airport to check out the ruins of **Panama Viejo**. There's not much left of the old city to see but a few piles of rocks so don't feel too bad if you find other things to interest you.

The city's suburbs, consisting of exclusive gated communities bursting with retirees and business executives, stretch out for miles in this direction. Construction cranes are ubiquitous. A nice side trip is a ride past former dictator **Noriega's** old house. It's a bit run down and not much to look at really but it's still a bit of history to see.

Needle-thin condo tours in **Paitilla** house the upper crust of Panama's wealth-hoarders and are a sight to see. Pedestrians share the streets with uniformed nannies taking cute kids out for a walk in their strollers. Glance around discreetly and you'll notice security-looking dudes lurking about with radios stuck in their ears. Behave.

Business and shopping districts like the area around **Vía España** are good for a quick look. If you must, visit the nearby **MultiCentro Mall**, which has all the usual consumer products, although it seems to be aimed at more upscale shoppers than I usually associate with.

For *molas*, you can't beat **Flory Saltzman's** shop in front of the Hotel El Panama anywhere in the country—even in the Kuna Yala where the Indian women who make these blouses come from. She and her mother have been dealing with these Indian ladies for decades and many of them bring her their best work. She has the best deals in the country and a vast selection.

In Panama, whenever you encounter ceviche on the menu, order it. For lunch, gorge on this wonderful food at **Mi Ranchito**, a sort of touristy place on the Amador Causeway. The food is *típico* with a twee folkloric band heaving away on weekends. I like the businessmen's expense account favorite: **Gaucho's** in the Calle Uruguay neighborhood. Of course steak is the star of the show, but they also have great ceviche and seafood entrees. See Chapter 11, *Best Sleeps & Eats,* for more details on these and other restaurants.

Your driver will certainly take you along Panama City's spectacular waterfront on **Vía Balboa**. The views are great and there is a wide sidewalk. Out to sea you can see dozens of ships milling about waiting for their turn through the canal. The city's wild skyline is on display. This is a **great photo spot**—just don't look down at the water or breathe

through your nose. There is no beach, just rocks littered with the city's sewage, which discharges directly into the bay at several points along this walk. I suggest you don't get out of the car—just drive along with the air-conditioning on and dig the view.

The **seafood market** is at the southern end of Vía Balboa and is well worth a look. The market is reasonably modern (doesn't smell too bad) and has an amazing array of sea life for sale. Many of the species on sale seem inedible to me but Panamanians love to eat wiggly squids, weird-looking sea snails and such.

The seafood market is just around the corner from the next area of interest. When pirates looted and destroyed Panama Viejo, **Casco Viejo**, now a **World Heritage Site**, became the new town site and walls and fortresses were built. The quaint old walled part of town crumbled almost to ruins until recent changes in demographics turned the area into the trendiest and artiest part of town. Slowly, the area is being restored to a point possibly beyond its former glory. Artsy types are remodeling old houses; trendy nightspots and even trendier restaurants are springing up all over the place.

I suggest a slow drive around the area with a stop or two at shops or to walk through the old church in the square. The area has still not been completely yuppified and is right next to one of the roughest parts of town. I still feel a little uneasy walking around the area on my own. Get the club or restaurant you are patronizing to call you a cab in the evenings. No matter what, do not miss having dinner at one of Panama's greatest restaurants: **Manolo Caracol**, located in an old

ALTERNATE PLAN
Stay just outside town at the upscale Intercontinental Playa Bonita and enjoy the pleasures of the beach in a location that's convenient to Panama City.

building in Casco Viejo. The atmosphere, food and presentation are quite original (see *Best Sleeps* for details). Delicious!

If you have time, a drive through **Balboa** and parts of the old **Canal Zone** is well worthwhile. **Cerro Ancón** dominates the area and a drive through **Quarry Heights** to the top reveals vistas of Panama City's skyline, the canal and surroundings.

If you simply must see something of the **Panama Canal** before you go (a very reasonable request), get your driver to take you a short way out of town to the **Miraflores Locks Visitor Center**. For visitors, this is really the best part of the entire canal system. You get to see the locks in action up close. Huge ships glide past just inches from your fingertips. There are informative displays and a gift shop with trinkets for sale. The restaurant is mildly awful but the view of canal operations from the tables is great.

Saturday Night

I suggest a fine dinner at either **Siete Mares** or **Eurasia**. Both are upscale, quiet and elegant. Siete Mares translates as "Seven Seas" so you know what's on the menu there. They specialize in fresh corvina (sea bass) served in a variety of interesting ways. Eurasia is perhaps a little trendier with a definite fusion of Pac rim flavors. I love the place. Every time, when I fly into Panama, just as I land in Panama City, I say to myself "I'm going to get to eat at Eurasia tonight!"

After dining finely, hit **Calle Uruguay** to sample the sounds at **Il Boccalino** and **Unplugged**. An intimate live music venue, **Havana Rumba** on Amador Causeway is a great place to hear local musicians putting down serious, traditional and contemporary Latin sounds to an appreciative, local audience. It's not really on the tourist circuit. It's not a place for dancing and loud conversation. People come to listen to the sounds. It's my favorite night out in Panama City.

Then, for the courageous, gambling and/or people watching at the **Casino Via Veneto** in the El Cangrejo district. It's glitzy gambling and girls, girls, girls after 11pm, or so they tell me.

See Chapter 11, *Best Sleeps & Eats,* and Chapter 12, *Best Activities,* for more details on these restaurants and nightlife choices.

Sunday

If you don't have to get out of town right away, there are several short activities to consider.

Miraflores Locks Visitor Center is close by and good for a two or three hour excursion. This is a nice way to get close to the canal for a ringside view of the lock action. It's a short cab ride out of town and has a plethora of exhibits on canal history and operations. The restaurant has a great view of the lock and the huge ships going by. Too bad about the food, though.

Don't bother with the much-touted **Mi Pueblito.** I find it to be an overrated, cheesy tourist attraction where examples of Panamanian crafts and folklore are found. There are embarrassing folklore shows and overpriced restaurants. Busloads of unfortunate tourists are herded through like sheep and fleeced as they pass.

Better, the 660-acre **Metropolitan Park** is within the city limits and is well known as a birding spot with over 220 species observed. You can expect to see both two- and three-toed sloths, squirrel monkeys and, if you are sharp-eyed, boa constrictors. Get a cab or ask your driver to take you there to spend an hour or two wandering the well-marked trails.

A WONDERFUL WEEK IN PANAMA CITY

Panama City, simply *Panamá* to locals, offers all the big city pleasures: modern infrastructure, throbbing nightlife, an amazingly vibrant business community, wonderful, world-class restaurants, elegant residential neighborhoods, fancy shopping districts—all with Latin American flavor to the max.

RECOMMENDED PLAN: Check in at the centrally-located **InterContinental Miramar**; hire a car and driver for sightseeing and exploration; enjoy big-city pleasures like fine dining, live music, glittery casinos and interesting bars.

Marbella & Punta Paitilla

This is more or less central Panama City, and is contiguous to Bella Vista and El Cangrejo. **Vía España** runs right through the middle of it all.

Panama City has a vast selection of hotels, from budget joints with three rooms to gleaming, big city business towers with hundreds of rooms and penthouse suites. You can spend almost any amount of money you want. In spite of this seeming plethora of hotels, do not assume you can simply pop into town and grab any hotel you want. Amazingly, all the hotels seem to be almost perpetually booked up. **Book well in advance.**

One of the better deals in town for a large, big city-type hotel with all the services is the **Intercontinental Crowne Plaza.** It used to be a Holiday Inn but has been extensively updated. Still, it is not as fancy as some of the other high-end lodging options.

The **InterContinental Miramar Panama** is a big city business hotel with all the goodies. The views out to sea and of the amazing Panama City skyline are tremendous. It is a busy place with helicopters buzzing about landing at their two heliports. I found service in the hotel and in the restaurants to be snappy. This is a very professional operation. The location is good if you are interested in carrying on in the clubs and bars of the Calle Uruguay entertainment district—it starts right across the street. You can crawl back to your hotel in the wee hours after a night of salsa and mojitos.

Some people rave about the **Bristol.** I find it to be rather stuffy, with a quaint, British feel and great ambiance. I like the place but found the service to be substandard.

Don't Miss ...

• **Amador Causeway** – Stroll around sampling the interesting seaside bars and restaurants.
• **Hot, Hot Nightlife** – Dance the night away to hot Latin beats.
• **World-Class Restaurants** – Pac Rim seafood marvels.
• **Panama Canal** – See titanic ships and marvelous engineering up close.
• **Casco Viejo** – World Heritage Site old town with Havana-like architecture.

You can certainly explore this part of Panama City on foot, utilizing the occasional cab. When the humidity gets to be a bit much, flag down a taxi and cool off on the way to your next destination.

A great way to enjoy a short stay in Panama City is to **hire an English-speaking driver**. You can hire almost any cab in town for $10 an hour, but most drivers speak only fair English, if any. See Chapter 12, *Best Activities* for driver/guide recommendations. Hiring such a guide can be cheaper than renting a car with *much* less hassle. You simply have the driver meet you in front of your hotel and drop you off wherever. Cool.

Be sure to have a stroll or a slow drive through the high-rise canyons of **Punta Paitilla**, where the rich and glamorous nest. Head towards the airport to marvel at the amoeba-like suburbs of high-walled, gated communities filled with retirees from North America and Europe and wealthy South Americans. It's pleasant there, but you can't actually see much of the fancy houses since high walls surround entire neighborhoods.

You will almost certainly end up viewing the remains of what was once Panama City, *Panamá Viejo*, Old Panama. There is certainly a lot of history here, but not much of it remains to be seen other than a few small piles of rocks and one or two rather larger piles of rocks. Nonetheless, the area is almost always full of tour buses and school groups wandering around the ruins reading the few informative placards dotted about.

Panama City's 660-acre **Metropolitan Park** is well known as a birding spot with over 220 species observed. You can also expect to see both two- and three-toed sloths, squirrel monkeys and, if you are sharp-eyed, boa constrictors. The park has easy-to-see populations of parrots, toucans and manakins.

While not exactly an international shopping destination, Panama City has one of the best shopping experiences in Latin America with plenty of modern, trendy stores. **Vía España** is considered to be the premier street in town for upscale shops interspersed with down-market, bargain emporiums.

There are two large, modern malls with dozens and dozens of shops. **Albrook Mall** is more or less across the street from the domestic airport in the old Canal Zone and next to the new, quite modern bus terminal. The **MultiCentro Mall** is more central, located on Avenida Balboa. Both malls have several levels of shops and the usual barfsome food court emporiums. There are banks, ATMs and lots of shops selling sunglasses and sports clothes.

Flory Saltzman Molas, just in front of Hotel El Panama, is the place to buy authentic *molas*. The prices are, for the most part, better than you will find in San Blas and the selection is incredible. There is no hard sell here. She has used or poor quality *molas* from $2.50. The really nice ones, sewn together into large wall hangings, can go for as much as a couple of hundred dollars. You can't go home without a bunch of molas to give to friends and family.

Panama Hats

Panama hats are often sought out by visiting gringos. While you certainly can buy lots of Panama hats in Panama, the best ones are actually made in Ecuador. The national hat of Panama is the slightly less stylish *sombrero pintado*, or "painted hat." These are great for keeping the sun out of your eyes. You will occasionally see a Panamanian wearing a Panama hat, but the vast majority of Panama hat wearers are visiting gringos. No problem.

The city has a wonderful, beautiful waterfront with wide boulevards running along the shore. The seaside sidewalks and parks are good for a tourist stroll and the spot to take pictures of the astounding Panama City skyline. Just don't look down into the water and see the untreated sewage spewing forth from the city behind, or take too deep a breath. Used condoms line the shoreline rocks and float ominously back and forth on the tide. Nice.

Dining in Panama City can mean choosing between fusions of a surprising number of cultures. Local seafood is tops. Add in influences from Spain, Asia and other Latin American countries and your selection of flavors to explore is fat.

Dark tile floors and wrought iron set the mood at one of my favorites, **Gaucho's** in the Calle Uruguay neighborhood. It's usually loud and bustling, full of businessmen on expense account lunches. If you want s seafood prepared in imaginative ways, try the intimate and romantic **Siete Mares**. Or go to my favorite restaurant in Panama City, **Eurasia**, one of the top restaurants in all of Panama. See Chapter 11, *Best Sleeps & Eats,* for more details on these and other great restaurants.

You have a wide choice of bars and nightlife in Panama City, including casinos (such as the **Veneto**). Be aware that the music and dance scene in Panama City is a very late night thing. Some clubs do not even open before 2am and may run wild until 8am or 9am in the morning. Clubs come and go. Hot clubs become cold clubs and disappear with regularity. See Chapter 12, *Best Activities,*for more details on nightlife activities.

Casco Viejo

By far the most interesting part of town architecturally, **Casco Viejo** drips with charm. The **World Heritage Site** neighborhood resembles Havana, but is being renovated, bit-by-bit. Trendy clubs, restaurants, bohemian-style apartments and the French Embassy make Casco Viejo one of the most up and coming neighborhoods in Panama City.

I suggest taking a taxi to and from the neighborhood. Although the area is rapidly gentrifying, there are still pockets of poverty. The nearby neighborhoods of Chorrillo and Santa Ana are appalling. Since the Casco Viejo area is blessed with beautiful old buildings worth renovating, investors long ago pushed up property prices far beyond anything the locals could handle. They are forced out as the gentrification process proceeds. This is, of course, happening all over other parts of the city also.

An hour or two spent exploring the old city walls and taking pictures of the Panama City skyline will pretty much cover things. Try to talk the guards at the ceremonial **Palacio Presidencial** into letting you look through the gates at the herons kept inside. It's quite impressive to see these big guys up close. They come right up to the gates to check you out. The palace is nice too.

A quick stroll through the old-fashioned **Plaza de la Independencia** should be undertaken. Discreetly walk through the **Catedral Metropolitana** where the desiccated remains of an obscure saint seem to have been secreted behind a painting of Jesus.

There are several good restaurants in trendy Casco Viejo. One stands out. **Manolo Caracol** does things sort of tapas style with a set meal of numerous courses. There is no menu—they just start bringing out great seafood, shellfish, snails, interesting vegetables and choice morsels of pork and other out of the ordinary items to gorge on. They have a great wine list with plenty of mouth-watering Spanish selections.

The trendiness of the area extends to nightlife. **La Casona de Las Brujas** features the latest in young, US-style rock. **La Platea** is *the* spot in Panama for jazz and salsa. See Chapter 11, *Best Sleeps & Eats,* and Chapter 12, *Best Activities,* for more details on these restaurants and nightlife choices.

Amador Causeway

When the Panama Canal was blasted out, huge rocks and other debris was piled up into a two-mile-long breakwater with gun emplacements and other massive concrete military accessories. Since it was turned over for municipal use, it has become Panama City's **top entertainment and recreation area.**

There are trendy clubs, restaurants, music venues and miles of paths for walking, biking and people watching. The view from the causeway over the bay to the dazzling Panama City skyline is *estupendo*!

Have dinner at your choice of eateries, and follow on with an evening in an intimate club for live music and adult beverages. It's hard to beat a night messing around on the Amador Causeway with your sweetie.

Mi Ranchito is a more or less *típico* restaurant with open sides so you can people watch, check out the view of the city and see the ships going by on the way to and from the canal.

If you have an uncontrollable urge to dance, dance, dance, the **Acqua Bar** on Amador Causeway boasts "world famous" DJs. Could be.

Perhaps the best bet for the over 30 crowd who love live music is **Havana Rumba**. Local musicians play to a mostly local crowd who are serious about listening to a dedicated musical group playing Latin classics. This is a very good evening out if you appreciate live music in an intimate setting.

See Chapter 11, *Best Sleeps & Eats,* and Chapter 12, *BestActivities,* for more details on these restaurants and nightlife choices.

4. THE PANAMA CANAL

Although a canal may sound boring, almost everyone enjoys the engineering marvel of the locks and lakes of the impressive Panama Canal. My wife says interest in the workings of the canal is a guy thing, but I disagree. It seems every visitor to Panama I meet, people of all ages and types, men and women, are fascinated with the history and present-day operations of the canal.

Many visitors to Panama never set foot on shore. A highlight of any southern cruise is the transit through the Panama Canal. The deck of a cruise ship is a spectacular way to view the locks, the lakes and the jungles that surround them.

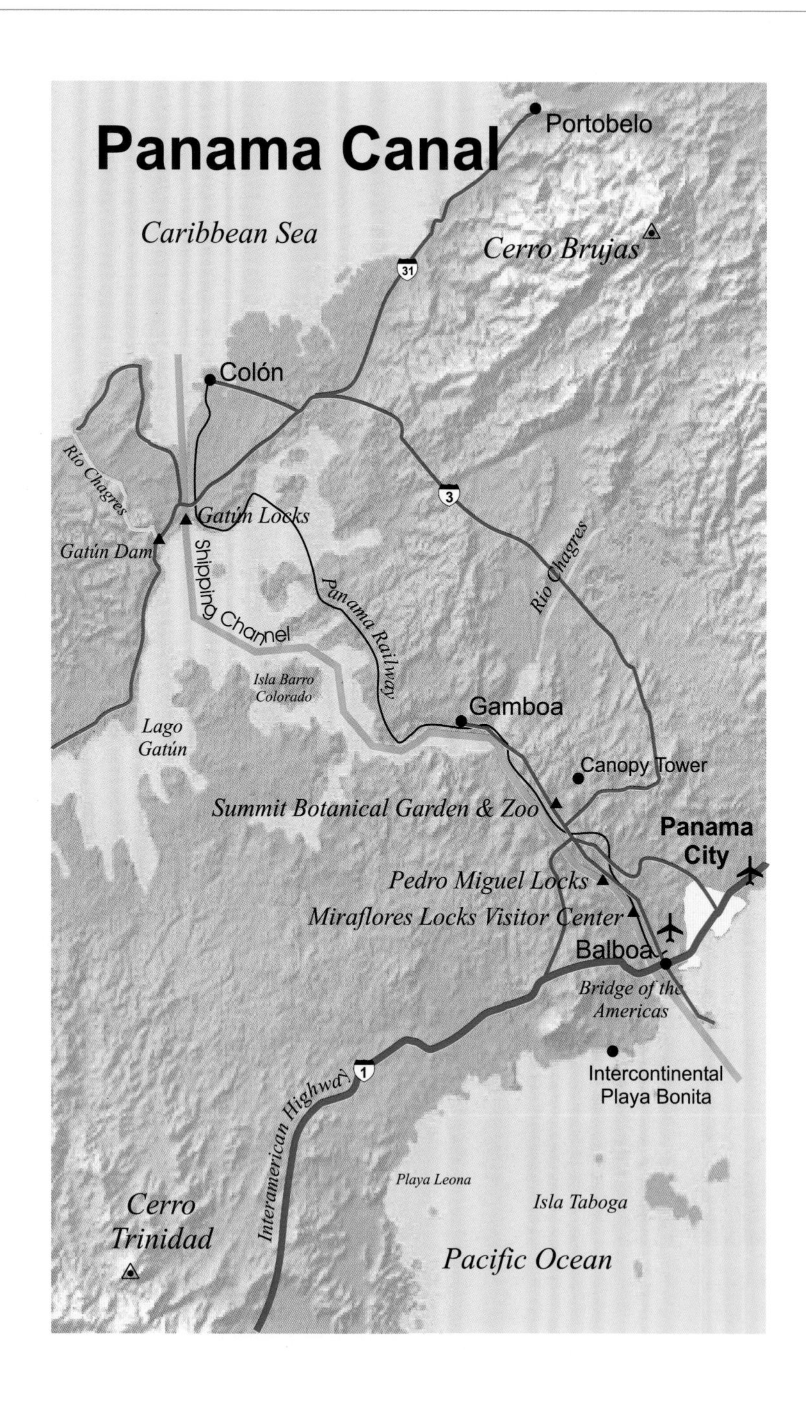
Panama Canal
Portobelo
Caribbean Sea
Cerro Brujas
31
Colón
3
Río Chagres
Gatún Locks
Gatún Dam
Shipping Channel
Panama Railway
Río Chagres
Isla Barro Colorado
Lago Gatún
Gamboa
Canopy Tower
Summit Botanical Garden & Zoo
Panama City
Pedro Miguel Locks
Miraflores Locks Visitor Center
Balboa
Bridge of the Americas
Intercontinental Playa Bonita
1
Interamerican Highway
Playa Leona
Isla Taboga
Cerro Trinidad
Pacific Ocean

ONE GREAT DAY AT THE PANAMA CANAL

If it's Saturday, you're all set. Full and half-transits of the canal are run on Saturdays only. Two companies offer half-day excursions on comfortable boats through the locks and Lake Gatún. This is perhaps the best way to see the canal and marvel at its inner workings.

If you don't fancy being on a boat half the day, hire a driver to take you around the old Canal Zone, along the canal itself, and to Miraflores Locks Visitor Center. You can also take the picturesque train along the edge of the canal from Balboa to Colón, or the other way.

Morning

Start the day driving over the attention-grabbing **Bridge of the Americas**. From the bridge, look out to sea where dozens of freighters, container ships and oil tankers wait for their turn to transit the canal. Drive back across the bridge, through Balboa and the old Canal Zone near Panama City.

Drive up **Cerro Ancon** through the old colonial officers' housing area **Quarry Heights** for a view of Panama City and the Canal Zone. You can see the busy port in action as you drive towards Miraflores.

It's a short drive from Balboa to **Miraflores Locks Visitor Center** where the spectacular locks are right at your feet. The observation decks give a bird's eye view of the whole operation. The **museum and exhibits** are quite good. The history and engineering of the canal are described in great detail in pictures and videos. They have a small **gift shop**. There is a basic lunchroom with a wonderful view of passing ships.

> **ALTERNATE PLAN**
> Take the old Panama Canal Railway Company train from near Balboa to Colón and hire a driver to drive you back along the canal, stopping at Gamboa and Summit Park for sightseeing. But don't linger in Colón, a dangerous slum. While a new cruise ship terminal, Colón 2000, has been built there to stir up the economy, the city remains unsafe and dirty. If you do find yourself on the streets of Colón, local residents themselves will likely come up to you and suggest getting out of town ASAP. Otherwise, expect to be mugged.

You may as well choke down lunch here, as there are really no particularly good places to eat nearby.

Afternoon

After a dire lunch at the **Miraflores Locks Visitor Center**, head north along the side of the canal to Gamboa where you can take a tour of **Lago Gatún** (*see photo below*) to see monkeys, sloths and exotic birds, and watch huge container ships slide along the lake portion of the canal. This is a great trip to take—don't miss it. **Ancon Expeditions** will arrange the whole thing for you, including transportation to and from Panama City if you need it. *Info*: *507-269-9415.*

After enjoying the lake, drive to **Gatún Locks** and the largest earthen dam in the world. If you have time, you can catch the old train from the seedy and insalubrious town of Colón, directly back along the banks of the canal to Balboa. This is a wonderful ride. Well worth the $25 ticket price.

Evening

Amador Causeway at night is a sight to behold. The lights of the Panama City skyline dazzle across the bay, and huge ships pass close by while you eat at one

of the romantic canal-side seafood joints. Mi Ranchito is a nice spot to have a romantic *típico* meal while enjoying the traditional tourist band.

A FANTASTIC PANAMA CANAL WEEKEND

Saturday is the day sightseeing transits of the canal are offered. Two companies have full and partial transits of the locks on picturesque tour boats. Lunch, drinks and discussions of hydraulic engineering are featured.

The former Canal Zone has a wide range of attractions other than the canal. Almost pristine secondary and primary **tropical forests** cover the area. Animal, bird and lovers of nature in general will find plenty to interest them, even after the obligatory canal trip.

Friday Evening

There are several quiet hotels and an excellent B&B in the area of the old Canal Zone adjacent to Panama City. I suggest the **Albrook Inn** or the comfortable B&B **La Estancia.** La Estancia is on the side of **Cerro Ancon** in the historic (used to be US Army Senior Officers housing) **Quarry Heights.** Birders can add to their life lists while sipping coffee on the balcony off the B&B's lounge. If you have good wind, you can walk up the hill to an observation point at the top of the hill and look out over the famous skyline of Panama City and out to the Pacific where dozens of huge ships wait their turn for the trip through the canal and its locks.

There are lots of interesting places to eat and stroll along the **Amador Causeway**. The

ALTERNATE PLAN

Stay at the more-or-less luxurious Gamboa Rainforest Lodge and explore the surrounding Soberanía National Park and Lake Gatún. The birding is some of the best in the world. The pool is nice too.

view of the legendary Panama City skyline is best enjoyed from this point of view. **Mi Ranchito** is a more or less *típico* restaurant with open sides, so you can enjoy being on the causeway and watch the ships go by.

Perhaps the best bet for the over-30 crowd who love live music is **Havana Rumba** on the Amador Causeway. Local musicians play to a mostly local crowd who are serious about listening to dedicated Latin musicians playing the classics. This is a very good evening out if you appreciate live music in an intimate setting. See Chapter 11, *Best Sleeps & Eats,* and Chapter 12, *BestActivities,* for more details on these restaurants and nightlife choices.

Saturday

You simply must do at least a **half transit of the canal**. The workings of the canal are impressive and best seen up close—from a boat on the canal itself. A half transit tour takes in two sets of locks and the most scenic and interesting areas of the canal in about a half-day. The full transit tour does the whole length of the canal and takes a long day. Both tours take place on Saturday only, but the full transit happens only once a month.

Although you get to see the whole enchilada on a tour that does the full transit of the canal, in my opinion that's a bit much. A full transit is a long day, and many hours of it are spent toddling along on Gatún Lake between Gatún Locks and the Pedro Miguel Locks. If your interest in the canal itself is strong, and you can schedule it, do the full transit or you'll regret it later. *Info*: Two companies offer the tours: **Canal & Bay Tours**, *Tel. 507-209-2009* and **Panamá Marine Adventures**, *Tel. 507-226-8917.* Both have interesting and comfortable boats with air-conditioned lounges and running commentary. Food and drink are available. You should call for departure times. The boats leave from a dock located almost under the Bridge of the Americas. The trip takes about five hours for half transits and ends up in Gamboa. Transportation back to Panama City is provided.

Next, visit the **Centro de Artesanías Internacional**, located by the YMCA in Balboa for basic tourist shopping. The center has stalls with handicrafts from around Panama with carvings, *molas*, and other traditional crafts. This is the place to buy a Panama hat. Prices start around $20 and go on up from there. You can pay over $200 for a particularly nice, soft and pliable Panama hat.

Skip the Free Trade Zone

Colón is home to the famous Zona Libre, an enormous duty-free trading and transshipment park where hundreds of international shippers, middlemen and wholesalers operate. There is nothing of interest there for tourists. Prices for the few things on sale to casual visitors are no better than you can get in stores in Panama City. Many visitors to Panama assume it would be a great place to shop, but it's not.

A visit to the 55,000-**Soberanía National Park** is a good choice for the rest of the afternoon. The park runs along the east side of the Panama Canal and consists of mountainous tropical rainforest with a well-developed trail system and the famous birding site, **Pipeline Road**. Over 400 bird species have been encountered in the 54,000-acre park.

ALTERNATE PLAN

If Balboa seems a little quiet to you and you want to sample something beyond the tourist delights of Amador Causeway, take the short cab ride into nearby Panama City for fine dining and nightlife.

If want a top-quality restaurant experience for Saturday night, your choices are limited to one of the seafood restaurants on **Amador Causeway**, the not-so-hot Lagarto in Gamboa, or one of the other restaurants at Gamboa Lodge. It's a short cab ride into Panama City, and fabulous, world-class restaurants like Eurasia or Manolo Caracol should not be missed. See Chapter 11, *Best Sleeps & Eats.*

Sunday

Go on the **Panama Canal Rainforest Boat Adventure** on Gatún Lake with Ancon Expeditions. Although they do not actually go through any locks, this tour takes in the wildlife around Lake Gatún with plenty of opportunities to view the huge Panamax freighters as they transit the canal. The tours leave from Gamboa and guests are picked up at their hotel and escorted throughout the day by a naturalist guide. *Info*: *www.anconexpeditions.com; Tel. 507-269-9415*

If you have any time left in the afternoon, **Summit**, a large park/zoo, is well worth a look. If you are a photographer, this is a good place to get up close to jaguars, toucans, harpy eagles and other exotics. You don't have to tell anyone back in Ardmore you took the shots at the zoo.

The famous birding site **Pipeline Road** is within **Soberanía National Park**. Over 400 bird species have been encountered in the 54,000-acre park. There are several roads and trails that can be appreciated by even a casual visitor.

> **ALTERNATE PLAN**
>
> Fishing for peacock bass on Lake Gatún is legendary. The fish are so plentiful, you can plan on catching hundreds of them up to 5 lbs. on a day out. This is a great trip for kids since they will be sure to land some. Trips leave from Gamboa. Check with Ancon Expeditions, *Tel. 507-269-9415.*

Mi Pueblito is a twee tourist attraction where cheesy examples of possibly Panamanian crafts and folklore are found. The folklore shows are littered with gringos gawking about in garish tourist outfits. If you've been herded like cattle on tour buses or cruise ships in the Caribbean or Latin America, you will probably have already been to a place just like this. Light the fuse and run. This one's a real stinker.

A WONDERFUL WEEK IN THE OLD CANAL ZONE

A week spent exploring the old Canal Zone area is time enough to admire the canal's amazing engineering and to marvel at the flourishing tropical rainforest and Lake Gatún. Don't miss wonderful birding around world-famous Canopy Tower. Amador Causeway throbs with nightlife, and world-class fine dining awaits in nearby Panama City.

RECOMMENDED PLAN: If you are staying for a week, you can choose one central location as a base for exploring the area or sample several lodging options in different areas—beach, jungle, or city. Taxis are relatively inexpensive and not a bad way to get around, especially in Balboa and nearby Panama City. **Hire a car** with a multi-lingual driver, which can be had for $10 to $12 per hour for more distant exploration. This is a great way to visit the canal and surrounding attractions.

Balboa

Balboa is nicely located in the tree-shaded old Canal Zone, yet is adjacent to Panama City—close enough to enjoy the fine dining and nightlife available there. I suggest checking into **La Estancia**, a comfortable and economical B&B on the slopes of Cerro Ancon. An alternative would be the **Intercontinental Playa Bonita**. It's only a mile or two from the canal but it is very quiet and isolated on its own long and picturesque beach.

The most charming of Panama's B&Bs, La Estancia is located on the slopes of Cerro Ancon overlooking the canal and the **Bridge of the Americas**. Monkeys, sloths and innumerable birds lurk just outside your bedroom window. It's very handy to Albrook airport if you need a handy place for the night between flights.
The area is part of the old US Army Senior Officers housing and the building has been remodeled and is up-to-date. Things are quiet here—it's completely residential. I prefer to stay somewhere quiet like this and take taxis into town.

The **Intercontinental Playa Bonita** would be a handy base for exploring the Canal Zone while enjoying the pleasures of a beachfront resort. I don't know how many pools they have—I kept losing count.

Don't Miss ...

- Amador Causeway – Stroll around sampling the interesting seaside bars and restaurants.
- Canal Transit – See the engineering marvels up close.
- Railroad Alongside the Canal – Ride in the observation car.
- Casco Viejo – In nearby Panama City, try Manolo Caracol.

The beach is of the interesting variety rather than the Miami Beach white sand type. The water is a little on the murky side and perhaps dodgy for swimming, actually.

For shopping, visit the **Centro de Artesanías Internacional**, located by the YMCA in Balboa. There are stalls with handicrafts from around Panama: carvings, molas, and other traditional crafts. This is the place to buy a Panama hat. Prices start around $20 and go on up from there.

You can pay over $200 for a particularly nice, soft and pliable Panama hat.

The **Panama Canal Railway Company** offers a wonderful trip along the canal banks on a charming and comfortable old train. Leaving from Corozal near Balboa, the picturesque Canal Zone-era train departs at 7:30am for the hour-long trip along the canal to Colón. The cars are very comfortable and there are great old-timey observation decks. The return trip gets into Corozal at 5:30pm. Realize that the destination town, Colón, is not a safe or interesting place for tourists. I suggest having a hired car with driver meet you at the station in Colón for a leisurely ride back to Panama City, taking in the numerous sights along the way. *Info: Tel. 507-317-6070.*

Two companies offer tours, **canal transits**, on appealing boats through the locks of the canal. They're great tours. Tours of the canal are either half- or full-day transits. On full transits, a major part of the day is spent motoring along through Lake Gatún, which is simply not as interesting as the portion of the transit spent passing through the locks. Half-day transits focus just on the locks nearer Panama City and are usually the best bet unless you are a retired engineer or otherwise canal-obsessed.

The *Pacific Queen,* run by **Panama Marine Adventures**, offers half-day partial canal transits with lunch in air-conditioned splendor on Saturdays for $99. It's a 5-hour trip and involves pickup and return to Amador Causeway. Once a month they do a full transit. *Info*: *Tel. 507-226-8917.*

Canal and Bay Tours has two boats doing canal transits both half- and full-day. They also run on Saturdays only and leave from Amador Causeway. *Info: Tel. 507-209-2009.*

Amador Causeway

Formed as a breakwater from debris from canal dredging, the causeway juts out two miles into the Pacific. Dozens of ships waiting to transit the canal lurk within sight. The stunning **Panama City skyline** is spectacular, especially at night. Dozens of entertainment-oriented **clubs**, **bars** and **restaurants** have sprung up. A few hotels exist, and more upscale resorts are planned. On weekends, it hums with activity as locals and tourists alike enjoy Panama City's newest entertainment district.

There are dozens of places to eat. Although a little on the touristy side, I like Mi Ranchito. It presents itself as a *típico* restaurant serving seafood, *patacones* and other Panamanian dishes. The food is okay, leaning towards shrimp and steak with rice.

Perhaps the best bet for the over 30 crowd who love live music is **Havana Rumba**, on the Amador Causeway. Latin musicians play to a mostly local crowd who are serious about listening to dedicated musicians playing the classics. This is a very good evening out if you appreciate live music in an intimate setting.

Gamboa

I suggest you stay at **Canopy Tower** (*see photo below*) for at least a couple/three nights and visit **Pipeline Road**, **Summit Gardens** and other birding and wildlife hot spots. Consider the Gamboa Resort's old Canal Company homes for a group—what a deal! If you have four or more people traveling together, you should look into renting one of the nicely remodeled old Canal Zone managers' houses left over from the US canal days that are part of the "luxury" **Gamboa Resort**. They are not particularly expensive and are quite comfortable and full of colonial charm. The location is, handily, about in the middle of the Canal Zone.

Canopy Tower is *the* mecca for hard-core birders. It is simply the **holiest birder shrine in the world**. The lodge is a converted radar tower on top of a hill in the middle of the rain forest. Rooms are on floors of the tower right at canopy level with the lounge/dining floor just above the canopy. The top deck has views for miles over the jungle of the **Soberanía National Park** and of the nearby Panama Canal. Visitors can view birds and wildlife at all levels of the surrounding rainforest.

The lodge employs some of the top bird guides on the planet to guide their guests to nearby holy spots like Pipeline Road, the Ammo Dump and Semaphore Hill.

Appealing to luxury vacation seekers and eco tourists alike, the **Gamboa Rainforest Lodge** is a large, deluxe lodge at the edge of the lush rainforest overlooking Gatún Lake. Even though this is not one of those rainforest ecolodges, the amount of wildlife surrounding you is simply amazing. In the morning, as you sip your coffee in your hammock on the balcony, the noise from thousands of birds drowns out normal conversation. They have an excellent serpentarium (snake house), orchid house, butterfly garden and lots of walks by the lake. It is a birding hot spot.

Lago Gatún is well known as a prime destination for landing dozens and dozens of **hard-fighting peacock bass**. The lake is absolutely bursting with them—so many that authorities encourage catching and keeping as many as anglers can boat. Some boat well over a hundred peacock bass up to 7 lbs. per person per day. Ancon Expeditions can arrange for half- or full-day fishing trips, usually leaving from the marina at Gamboa.

Lake Gatún is a huge lake formed when the canal was built. Canal traffic passes spectacularly through the jungle-surrounded lake.

The best way to enjoy this ecologically unique area is to take the **Panama Canal Rainforest Boat Adventure** offered by Ancon Expeditions. It sounds touristy but it is actually quite an in-depth and informative trip through the tropical forests and islands in and around the lake. Sloths, monkeys, birds, crocs, all the expected jungle wildlife is right in your face. The awning covered boats get right up next to things. These guys really do a good job.

A large park/zoo, **Summit** is not as depressing as most zoos. They have a large variety of wildlife and a stunning **jaguar exhibition**. The cats sometimes stalk aggressively around their enclosures, bellowing at visitors. The harpy eagle exhibit had only two birds the last time I was there and they were a bit hard to see.

The 55,000-acre **Soberanía National Park** runs along the east side of the Panama Canal and consists of mountainous tropical rainforest. It has well developed trails, and two resorts bordering it. The famous birding site **Pipeline Road** is within the park. There are several roads and trails that can be appreciated by even a casual visitor.

Birding in the canal area is exceptional by any standard. It includes several of the top birding destinations in the world. Top-quality guides are available who can satisfy even the most experienced birders.

With a list exceeding 400 species, **Pipeline Road,** an overgrown maintenance road, is the best place in the world to see tropical forest bird species. You can drive along some of it but walking, very early in the morning is the holiest way to behave on Pipeline Road. With luck, you might see a sapayoa, buff-rumped warbler, dull-mantled antbird or even a crake or resplendent quetzal (*see photo on next page*).

If you must, visit **Summit Golf Club**, which has a wonderful clubhouse dripping with colonial charm and a modern 18-hole course designed by Jeffrey Myers. The place has been around forever and is loaded with colonial-era charm.

5. BOCAS DEL TORO

Bocas del Toro is probably the best-known tourist destination in Panama. It is a beautiful Caribbean paradise of small islands and coral reefs. Remote, luxury lodges waaay out in the islands compete with backpacker hostels in heaving Bocas Town, which is filthy with backpackers, yachties, surfers and retired gringos looking for fun. Booming reggae music never stops. Seedy bars and tropical dives lure the adventurous. Young counter-culture North Americans with their hair in faux dreadlocks snort coke and puff grass. Down-at-the-heels gringos bend your ear in bars hoping to cadge a free drink or sell you some real estate. I love the place. The archipelago is remote. You can only get there by plane or boat.

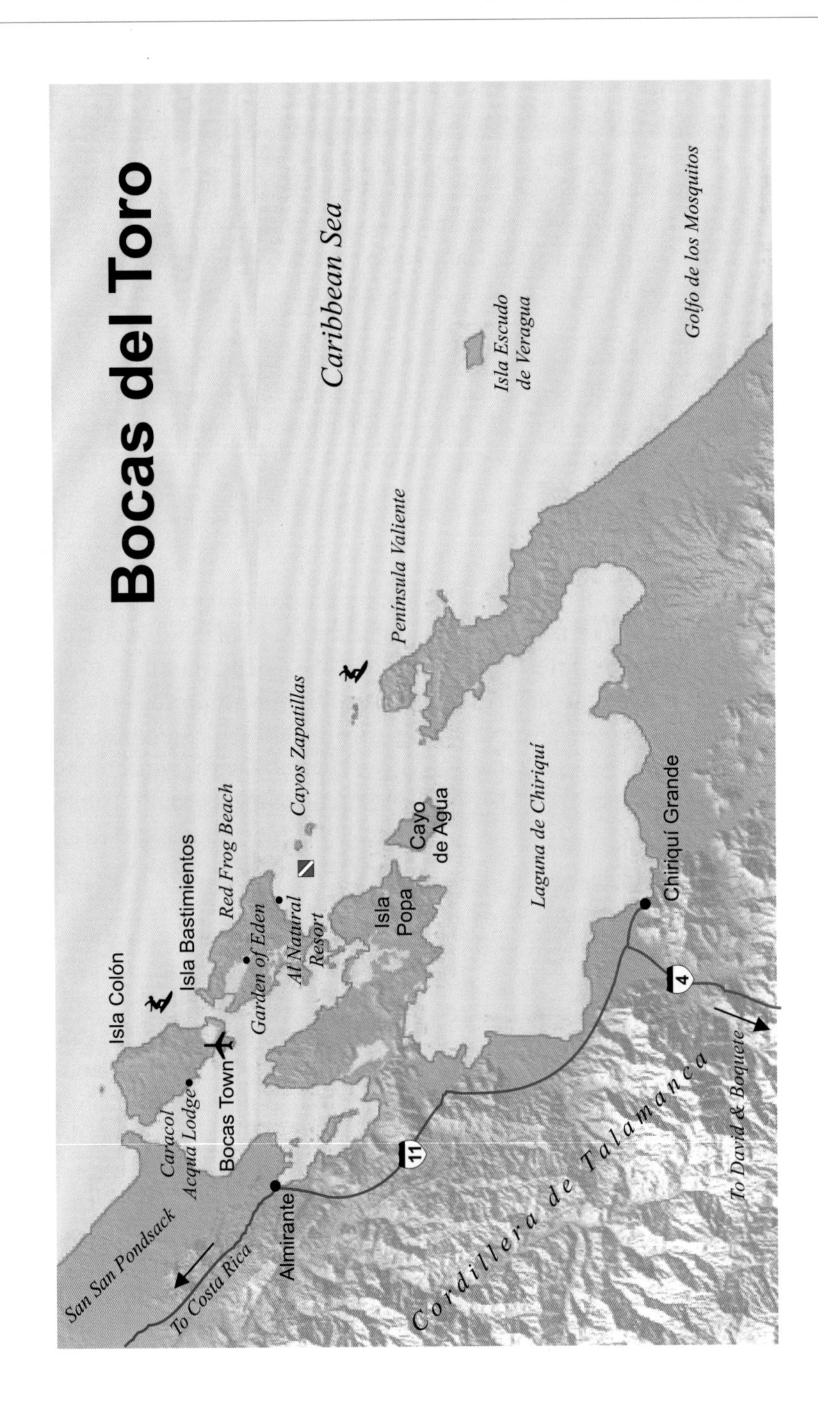
Bocas del Toro
Caribbean Sea
Isla Escudo de Veragua
Golfo de los Mosquitos
Península Valiente
Cayos Zapatillas
Red Frog Beach
Isla Colón
Isla Bastimientos
Garden of Eden
Al Natural Resort
Isla Popa
Cayo de Agua
Laguna de Chiriquí
Chiriquí Grande
4
To David & Boquete
Cordillera de Talamanca
11
Bocas Town
Caracol Acqua Lodge
San San Pondsack
To Costa Rica
Almirante

ONE GREAT DAY IN BOCAS DEL TORO

Unless you come by cruise ship, Bocas del Toro is not easily visited in one day. There are no roads to it, and it is at the extreme northwestern end of the country next to the Costa Rican border. You have to take a boat or fly to get there.

If you are fortunate enough to be on a cruise ship that stops here, you'll be taken around sightseeing to snorkeling spots and scenic beaches by small boat and dropped off in town to shop for tourist trinkets and sample the bars. Enjoy.

Morning

You can hire a boat for tours of the remote islands at Jampan Tours, and you simply must get out of town to admire the beauty of the surrounding islands and reefs. If the Robinson Crusoe life appeals, they'll take you to a remote tropical paradise, **Cayos Zapatillas**, and drop you off with lunch and a cooler. These charming, tiny islands are picture-postcard perfect with white sand encircling coconut palms. The snorkeling is great.

ALTERNATE PLAN

Catch a water taxi for $2 to nearby Bastamientos Town, where the reggae lifestyle predominates. Dogs meander around dusty paths. There are laid back bars overlooking the water for consuming soothing tropical beverages.

Afternoon

Drift around funky Bocas Town checking out the **cheesy shops** and **"interesting" bars**. There are a number of good restaurants and seaside watering holes with decks overlooking the teeming Bocas waterfront. Like everyone else here, take some time to gaze over the island with a cool beverage in hand.

Vendors congregate around the meager park, selling flyblown street food and hippie beads. Street front shops sell ice cream to water bottle-clutching tourists. Little stalls at the north end of Calle 3 sell molas and low-end tourist items. Once you have circled the square and strolled up and down both Calles 1 and 3, you've pretty much done the town.

I suggest spending any remaining time at **El Limbo On the Sea** or **Lemon Grass** snacking on seafood and downing the interesting tropical concoctions dreamed up by the bartenders in these waterside watering holes. The music is usually not too loud and the food at both places is good.

Evening

Enjoy exotic Indian curries and lassis at **Om Café** in Bocas Town. This is really the most interesting restaurant in town, and the food is delicious. After dinner, wander around the streets checking out likely looking bars. Indulge in tropical adult beverages and crazy music. I suggest the **Barco Hundido** for over-the-top partying. It's great, it's loud and it goes on all night.

See Chapter 11, *Best Sleeps & Eats,* and Chapter 12, *BestActivities,* for more details on these restaurants and nightlife choices.

A FANTASTIC BOCAS DEL TORO WEEKEND

Don't stay in rowdy Bocas Town. There are several wonderful, quiet resorts within a $2 water taxi ride of the festering party town and more even further away on remote island paradises. Whatever you do, find any excuse to travel by boat to some of the remote, outlying islands to snorkel, fish, surf or just laze around. Go into Bocas at night for great seafood restaurants and hardcore partying.

Friday Evening

Take a water taxi to your remote luxury lodge. Check in, dump your bags, slide on your bathing suit and wade into the water to wiggle your toes in the sand. Start enjoying tropical fruit/rum concoctions as soon as you can in preparation for a wonderful seafood dinner. Get to know the other guests, marvel at the stars and phosphorescent water and polish off a few more adult beverages.

Saturday

Sleep as late as you can with the sea breeze blowing through, pull on a T-shirt and stroll to the lounge area of your lodge for a breakfast of toasted Johnnycakes, pineapple, papaya and other tropical goodies.

Dope?

Grass? Coke? Real Estate? So run the pitches as you walk by the park in Bocas Town. According to rumor, it's snowing in Bocas, but the police presence is uncooperative with a doper lifestyle. They bust pot smokers as well as anyone doing the hard stuff.

With snorkeling gear, cooler and a packed lunch, take a boat to **Cayos Zapatillas** to be dropped off for a few hours on a beautiful tropical isle. Postcard beautiful, these two gems are surrounded by clear water, coral reefs and colorful fish. There's nothing on the islands but palm trees and sand. You can run around naked all day if you like. Don't burn your bum.

Return to your lodge after your island lunch and either laze around or hike through the forest looking for **poison dart frogs**. In the early evening, get a boat ride into Bocas Town where you can wander around the seedy and touristy streets looking for interesting bars and musical happenings. **Barco Hundido** is famous for late night high jinks. **Bum Fuck's** (Baumfaulk's) also has a reputation for entertaining visiting gringos. Don't worry, it's a more-or-less straight bar.

ALTERNATE PLAN

Stay put. Spend the entire weekend piddling around your remote luxury lodge (like Al Natural, below) enjoying the beach, kayaking, snorkeling, eating and drinking. Lounge around in hammocks reading cheap novels.

Sunday

Spend your last morning enjoying one or more of the area's impressive beaches. There are several beautiful sand beaches and the surfing is great. The best waves generally arrive December through March; although nearby storms can kick things up nicely from time to time all year. **Red Frog Beach** is perhaps the most famous spot but The Dumps, Playa Punch and Playa Primera offer waves to challenge even jaded surfers.

If you end up in Bocas Town Sunday afternoon with a couple of hours to kill, there are several mellow waterfront bars/restaurants perfect for wasting a few hours. I suggest **Lemon Grass** (*see Best Sleeps & Eats*) for a casual spot to relax with a cold beverage and snacks while watching the insect-like water taxis zoom all around the waterfront.

A WONDERFUL WEEK IN BOCAS DEL TORO

Bocas del Toro has the beauty of **secluded tropical islands** with palm trees and beaches along with a heaving **counter-culture nightlife**. You can be a mellow ecotraveler in the daytime and a rowdy twenty-something gone wild at night.

RECOMMENDED PLAN: Don't stay in noisy Bocas Town unless you are a really hard-core partier. It's a great town, but the **very, very loud music from the bars goes on all night**. Literally. Instead, **select a luxury lodge** located on one of the isolated beaches scattered around the islands. Enjoy the natural beauty of the area and head for Bocas Town only when you need a fix of interesting seafood restaurants and crazy-ass bars. This could be every night.

Don't Miss ...

- **Rowdy Partying in Bocas Town** – Dance all night to hot DJ sounds.
- **Cayos Zapatillas** – Strand yourself on a palm-fringed tropical islet.
- **Doing Nothing!** – Enjoy world-class laziness as your hammock swings in the tropical tradewinds.
- **Surfing Red Frog** – Bocas is the #1 surf destination in Panama with dozens of challenging breaks.
- **Hot, Hot Vindaloo** – Om Cafe serves hip, hot and trendy Indian cuisine.

Bocas Town

Nightlife and entertainment are what Bocas Town is all about. The place heaves with bars and loud music emporiums pumping out drinks and trendy music every night until past dawn. The hottest, trendiest spots change, so check with your lodge or hotel for recommendations about the newest and best place to get smashed. Getting smashed is pretty much what it's all about. Avoid watermelon mojitos.

I suggest **Bocas Inn** if you intend to stay right in town. The hotel, clean and air-conditioned, is one of the nicest available in town and is only a few hundred feet away from the noisiest bars. See *Best Sleeps & Eats.*

Bum Fuck's is named after its colorful owner Bill Baumfaulk. The usual crowd includes visiting and local gringos mixed with a few young locals looking for gringo friends. It's loud, it's cool. It's great. Everyone calls it Bum Fuck's.

Another favorite is the **Barco Hundido**. It's a bar built on pilings and an adjacent barge. Apparently, the original bar sank at the dock, so they just opened a new one above it on pilings. The place rocks. Most of the action starts after midnight. It's built on and over the water with a large, floating bar on some sort of barge that has its own outboard motor. Reportedly, the owner gets into things himself from time to time and quietly unhooks the barge/ bar from the dock and takes revelers off into the islands on an impromptu booze cruise.

Bastamientos

Bastamientos is a large island immediately adjacent to Bocas Town. It has a very sleepy village and a couple of dozen lodging choices. There are a couple of happening bars on the waterfront opposite Bocas Town.

Coral Reefs

Coral is a communal organism. The colorful formations you see are colonies of thousands of tiny animals, which filter food from the water. The calcium they secrete builds a coral reef over hundreds of years. The coral attracts tiny fish and crustaceans, which attract larger predators, and so up the scale. A living reef is an incredibly complex ecosystem, which provides habitat for many important fish species. Pollution, sedimentation and overfishing chip away at the reefs. Rising sea temperatures are killing reefs in many areas and, worse yet, scientists now fear that, as absorbed carbon dioxide changes the chemistry of seawater, corals' very ability to produce calcium could be impaired. Whatever the future holds, Panama's reefs are beautiful now, so get out and enjoy them!

Sand Fleas, Anyone?

Many Panamanian beaches are thick with irritating sand fleas, almost invisible little buggers that swarm around the beach. Many people have their favorite sauces to drive away the little ankle-biters but, to my knowledge, none of these spreads works for everyone. Many swear by Avon's Skin-So-Soft, so it's a good idea to bring some as well as the usual DEET mosquito repellant.

You'll see tourists jumping into the water and splashing about in front of the seaside bars and hotels. Several have slides and other water toys to facilitate this. Realize that all of the hundred or so bars, restaurants and other businesses fronting the water pipe their waste streams (toilets) directly into this same seemingly inviting sea. Gross.

I have three favorite places to stay in this area. **The Garden of Eden** is a small, B&B run by a friendly couple from the Florida Keys on a tiny island all by itself. It's newish, very private, discreet, and moderately luxurious. A bit funkier is the wonderful **Al Natural**. Their casitas are open-air jobs with thatched roofs and the trade winds blowing through. They are on a small white sand beach and nicely located for walks all over the island. World-famous **Punta Caracol Acqua Lodge** (*photo below*) consists of thatched roof cottages built over the sea, reached by long catwalks. It is extremely picturesque. See *Best Sleeps & Eats* for more details on all of these places.

On Bastamientos, **Red Frog Beach** (*see photo below*) is perhaps the most famous surf spot but Dumpers, Playa Punch and Playa Primera offer waves to challenge jaded surfers. **Parque Nacional Marino Isla Bastamientos** protects large areas of Isla Bastamientos and the nearby underwater reefs. Some snorkeling spots are marked and have buoys for tying boats.

Bocas is wonderful for **kayaking**. The area around Bocas town teems with boat traffic, and wakes can be a problem. Bastamientos has several wonderful kayaking areas. Many of the lodges have kayaks for guest use.

Trolling for tuna from local dugouts or small outboards can be productive. Most of the time anglers can expect to nail a kingfish or two, a couple of snapper and some jack or needlefish, but the fishery has not been explored or developed for visitors to enjoy.

Cayos Zapatillas

These two tiny islets are picture postcard perfect with white sand and a few coconut palm trees. This is a good spot for a picnic or romantic interlude.

San San Pond Sack Swamp

These **wetlands** are a major draw for birders and nature lovers. Nearby Isla Escudo de Veraguas is the only place on the planet where you can find the tiny **Escudo hummingbird**. Swan Cay, *Isla Pájaros,* hosts the only Caribbean breeding colony of the red-billed tropicbird. Ancon Expeditions at the Bocas Inn can set you up with boats and guides.

6. SAN BLAS ARCHIPELAGO

One word sums up both the San Blas Islands and the colorful Kuna Indians who live there: photogenic. It's simply one of the most beautiful archipelagos anywhere. Small, white sand-rimmed islands with cute clusters of coconut palms by the hundreds dot the crystal clear and shallow water. The locals live a fairly traditional lifestyle and the women dress in one of the most colorful native outfits of any indigenous people, anywhere in the world.

There is actually not too much to do in the Kuna Yala other than lounge around on picturesque tropical islands and snorkel. But that's plenty. Be sure to get in plenty of time hopping from island to island by local water taxi. You'll take hundreds of pictures of beautiful island scenery, but only a few shots of the colorful natives, as they are rather strict about collecting $1 per click. Video cameras in Kuna villages are not on, unless you're ready to pay $60 or more.

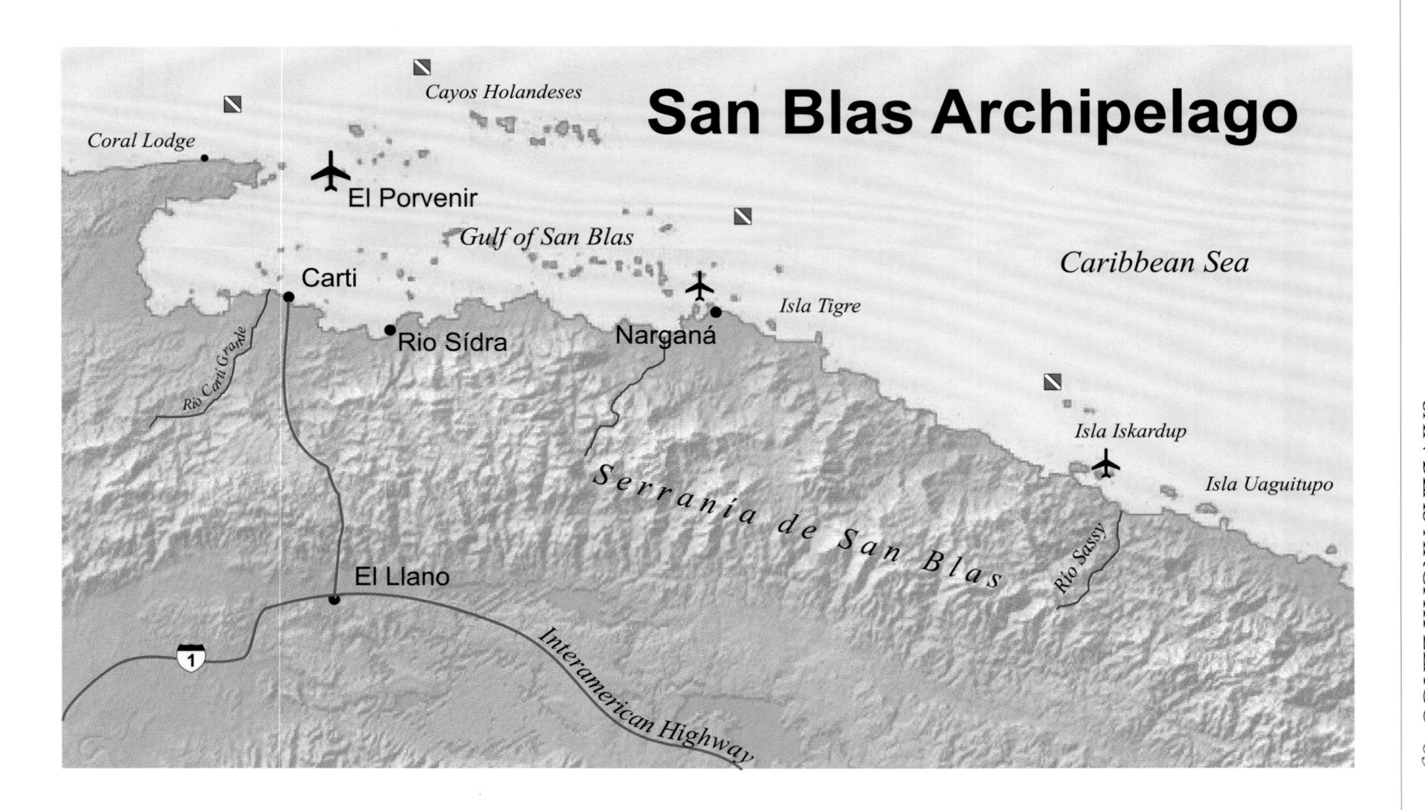
San Blas Archipelago
Cayos Holandeses
Coral Lodge
El Porvenir
Gulf of San Blas
Caribbean Sea
Carti
Isla Tigre
Rio Sídra
Narganá
Rio Carti Grande
Isla Iskardup
Isla Uaguitupo
Serranía de San Blas
Rio Sassy
El Llano
1
Interamerican Highway

A FANTASTIC SAN BLAS WEEKEND

If you don't want to rough it in the bare-bones accommodations within the borders of the Kuna Yala, right next door is luxurious Coral Lodge. They take guests on boat trips through the islands to visit remote Indian villages and enjoy the beautiful tropical islands set in sparkling Caribbean waters.

Friday Evening

Assume a late afternoon arrival at El Porvenir, either by charter flight or by car and boat. **Coral Lodge** (*see photo below*) will send a boat and guide to pick you up and take you for a visit to nearby **Corbisky Island**. There you can soak up local **Kuna Indian** culture strolling through the jam-packed native village. Women offer bright molas for sale and small girls in traditional dress pose for pictures with puppies or parrots.

When you've had your fill of native life and molas, you'll be whisked to Coral Lodge to your cabin over the water on the reef. The lodge is luxurious and isolated, just outside the Kuna Yala, and allows guests to be active hiking, kayaking, diving and surfing or just lying about the pool and beach. I love the place. They have a lovely thatched bohío over the water where meals and drinks are served.

Saturday

Slurp down a wonderful hot breakfast while seated over the lagoon. Colorful reef fish flit about as you enjoy your eggs and *patacones*. Ease into your day by snorkeling around the bay in front of the lodge for a little while, then rinse off in the shower and head to some of the more remote islands in the San Blas.

A few hours on tiny (about the size of a football field) **Dog Island** can be profitably spent snorkeling, lazing around in the shallow waters and drinking beer. There's not much else to do on the island. A small hut houses local Kunas who will sell you *molas* and other handicrafts.

The islands to the East are less visited and can be more interesting than the much visited El Porvenir and Corbisky. Boat trips can take an hour or more but the scenery along the way is stunning. **Isla Tigre** is cleaner than most of the other Kuna villages and is well worth a visit. Again, there is not much to do here but observe the locals going about their business, shop for molas and take pictures ($1 per snap). The water is waaay too polluted to swim and there really are no bars or other places to hang out.

Sunday

After a leisurely breakfast, a quick boat trip to Miramar in the lodge's launch is the first step on the way back to civilization. Next is an overland drive by 4WD to Portobello for a quick look at the ruins and a nice lunch at Coco Plum. After lunch, you can either drive back to Panama City or take the picturesque train ride from Colón, alongside the canal, back to town.

ALTERNATE PLAN

Get Elias Perez to arrange a kayak/camping trip through the eastern end of the San Blas, stopping at out of the way, exotic tropical isles. *Info*: *Corbisky Island. Tel. 507-6708-5254.*

A WONDERFUL WEEK IN SAN BLAS

Unless you have a private yacht, there are currently only two practical ways to see the San Blas Archipelago. One is to check into the wonderful and luxurious **Coral Lodge**, located at the edge of the **Kuna Yala**, and take day trips by boat to remote islands. The other way is to bum your way on the cheap from small island to small island, camping or staying in hammocks with local Indian families and in small "guesthouses" found on a few of the islands.

RECOMMENDED PLAN: To be able to see most of the remarkably picturesque San Blas Archipelago and to enjoy its pleasures to the fullest, I suggest staying at the isolated and luxurious **Coral Lodge**. The lodge is located at the western edge of the Kuna Yala and currently is the only comfortable place to stay in the entire province. Their multilingual guides will take you by boat to the most interesting **Kuna islands** and to the most picturesque tropic isles.

Kuna Yala

The Kuna Yala is a province of Panama run more or less autonomously by the Kuna Indians. The San Blas Archipelago is a group of islands within the Kuna Yala. The **Kuna Indians** control their area tightly, not allowing outsiders to live or do business within their borders. Life is vaguely traditional. Women still dress in colorful traditional garb but men dress as Western as they can afford. There are no tourist facilities other than the most basic, rustic type imaginable. Food served to outsiders is dreadful and expensive.

El Porvenir

El Porvenir is a crummy little town with a couple of rough buildings, a police station and a much-patched airstrip. Commercial flights land here, but there's really not much of interest. You have to check in with the police upon arriving, but it's a pretty casual deal. They write your passport details down in a spiral notebook. It is best to make arrangements in advance to be met here by the launch from Coral Lodge.

Sometimes the ride from El Porvenir to Coral Lodge involves a stop for a meal and a stroll around the Indian village on Corbisky Island.

Corbisky Island

Corbisky is just a half-mile or so from El Porvenir. It is a tiny island covered completely with the small bamboo, wood and tin shacks of the Kunas. **Elias Perez**, a Kuna who runs a small tour business, lives here and shows visitors around the islands. His wife is happy to sell you her wonderful *molas* (as are virtually all women in the area). She will quickly pull out dozens of them for you to choose from. *Info*: *Tel. 507-6708-5254.*

> **Don't Miss ...**
>
> • Shopping For Molas – Kuna women make and sell these brightly colored handicrafts.
>
> • Snorkeling Crystal Clear Waters Around Remote Islands – See beautiful reef fish and brightly colored coral.
>
> • Kayaking through the mangroves and over the coral reefs – Sneak up on wildlife in your silent kayak.

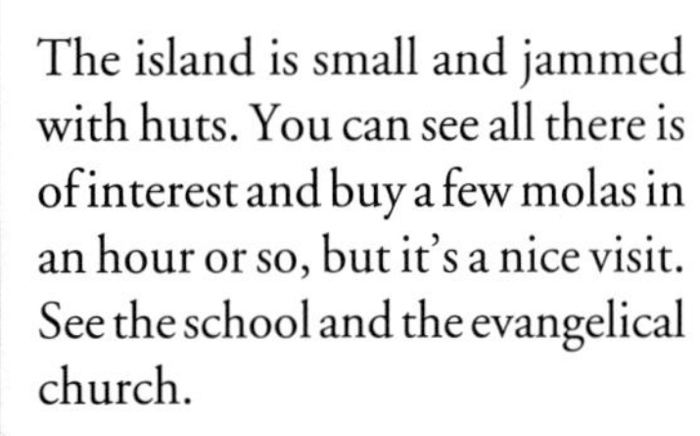

The island is small and jammed with huts. You can see all there is of interest and buy a few molas in an hour or so, but it's a nice visit. See the school and the evangelical church.

When I was last here, I spied a small girl in outrageously colorful traditional dress holding two tiny, squealing puppies posed cutely and conveniently by the path. Her mother, lurking nearby, cheerfully accepted a dollar for the picture I had to take. Not a

Getting Naked

Everybody always wants to know if it's okay to go around naked on the beaches in Panama. It's not. Panamanians are generally a conservative lot and dress well at all times—even at the beach. Most hotels will not tolerate nudity in and around their pools. So, no topless sunbathing, and leave the thong in your suitcase unless everyone else at your hotel pool is letting their stuff hang out.

bad deal for both sides of the transaction.

Coral Lodge

You don't really need shoes here. Straight off the cover of a travel magazine, the lodge is set in a coral-rimmed cove with curving sand beach and arching coconut palms. The setting is dramatic and the colors of the Caribbean Sea and sky are almost overwhelming. You can swim from your room to breakfast in a bohío perched on the reef. Romantic casitas are at the end of a long dock *waaay* out on the reef.

It is surprising that the promised luxury can be delivered this far out in the middle of nowhere, but they have the luxury part well covered. Meals are top-quality with seafood, steaks and local produce with good wines and good-quality spirits available.

The casitas are large and fairly private with hot water and air-conditioning. I spent several days lounging around in #4 and loved it. I would hop into the water from my private deck and snork around for short trips through the reef, then return to my casita for a quick shower and another sustaining beverage. Luxury.
The lodge is a good base for exploring the nearby San Blas Archipelago, allowing you to stay in luxury at night. The lodge's launches are used to take visitors through the islands and to visit Indian villages on daylong tours.

The manager is a certified PADI diving instructor. He is enthusiastic about sharing the magnificent offshore reefs with guests, and offers a full basket of certification programs. Well-preserved barrier reefs are just offshore from the lodge, and the diving is great.

Isla Tigre

Cleaner than most of the other Kuna villages and well worth a visit, **Isla Tigre** is a tiny speck of tropical paradise. It's the size of a football field, with white sand and coconut palm trees. There is a small Kuna hut where two brothers hang out. The snorkeling is good but there's not much else to do other than simply veg out.

Eastern Islands

The Kunas do not allow any scuba diving in their waters but the snorkeling can be good up and down the archipelago. Small out islands can be good spots for snorkeling. I suggest you refrain from snorkeling near any Kuna settlement since they discharge all waste directly into the waters around their homes. Not healthy for swimmers.

The Kuna do a good job of hoovering the seas around them and sucking up anything edible. As a result, fishing in the area is only fair. Unfortunately, the locals have a reputation for using bleach and other chemicals to flush lobster, squid, crab and other edibles out of their reef nooks and crannies into their awaiting nets.

The mangroves and offshore islands of San Blas are home to **numerous bird species** including anhingas, bare-throated tiger herons, wood storks and yellow-crowned night herons. The San Blas islands have a comparatively low density of bird species compared to other parts of Panama, but the Kuna Yala mainland is, for all practical purposes, inaccessible and has not really been explored thoroughly by birders. There are no qualified local guides although nationally recognized bird guides can help more adventurous groups navigate in the area.

7. THE GULF OF CHIRIQUÍ

The curve of Panama's Pacific coast creates a huge gulf studded with coral reefs and a few tropical islands, stunning in their beauty. Palm trees shade quiet, white sand beaches and huge waves bash against the rocks on the seaward side of the islands. The Gulf of Chiriquí is filthy with whales, billfish and seabirds disporting themselves for your viewing pleasure. You can surf, fish, scuba, watch whales or simply lounge around in the tropical beauty.

David
Cordillera Central
1
Pedregal
El Cruce
Puerto Armuelles
Boca Brava
Panamá Big Game
Playa Las Lajas
Santiago
Parque Nacional Marino Golfo de Chiriquí
Morro Negrito
Punta Burrica
Islas Secas
Islas Ladrones
Pacific Ocean
Golfo de Montijo
Isla de Coiba
Isla Montuosa
Parque Nacional Coiba
Gulf of Chiriquí
Isla Jicaron

A FANTASTIC GULF OF CHIRIQUÍ WEEKEND

A weekend is just enough time to get a good taste of the fantastic beauty of the gulf and **enjoy angling unmatched almost anywhere.** In fact, fishing for two days, you have an excellent chance of landing a few sailfish, tuna, dorado, wahoo, roosterfish and a marlin or two. If fishing isn't your thing, **whale watching** or just hanging out on a beautiful beach will prove equally enjoyable!

Friday Evening

Fly into David as early as possible on Friday. One of the guys from **Panama Big Game** will meet you for the short trip to the dock in Pedregal. From there, it's an hour-long boat ride to the remote lodge. The boat ride from Pedregal, through the mangroves, past **Wahoo Willie's** bar to **Boca Brava** is a wildlife tour in itself. When you land at the dock, you, your luggage, and supplies of all types go up to your rooms on an electric tram. No hassle. Save your breath for hauling in tuna tomorrow.

Hang around the bar and tell lies. Meals are served in the bar/lounge area and guests compete with manager Captain Lee to tell the wildest fishing stories. It's usually safe to ignore the other anglers and listen to your host, Captain Lee—he knows how to fish here.

The food is great, as Lee used to be a top chef in South Florida. There are always hot snacks, ceviche and sushi on the bar. Drink is included. So eat, drink, hang with your pals and go to bed early.

Saturday

The day starts with a knock on your door and coffee on a tray at about 5:30am. No problem.

Gorge on a full hot breakfast and get down to the boats at the crack of dawn, ready for a day out in the Gulf.

As the boat threads through the rocks and sand bars at the mouth of the Boca Brava, keep your eyes peeled for **humpback whales** breaching, doing headstands, smacking the surface of the water with their flukes and generally acting frisky. There are zillions of them concentrated in the Gulf pursuing their regular whale activities.

The waters around the spectacular islands in the gulf, **Montuoso**, **Islas Ladrones**, **Islas Secas** and others are fishing grounds almost without parallel in the world. The islands are really the tips of underwater mountains. Deep cold currents from the south meet underwater mountain ranges, creating rich plankton soup that attracts sea life in huge abundance.

This means that fishing for pelagics like **marlin**, **sailfish** and **yellowfin tuna**, along with inshore species like **snapper**, **roosterfish** and **grouper**, is simply brilliant. I have spent several days fishing with Captain Tati at Panama Big Game and can attest to the spectacular fishing. We caught dozens of wahoo, tuna, dorado and snapper and several marlin. Can't beat that.

ALTERNATE PLAN

Fly direct from Panama City to remote paradise Islas Secas and land at their private jungle airstrip. Spend the weekend soaking up the luxury, enjoying true 5-star meals, surfing, whale watching and lying around under the palm trees.

The boats usually return to the dock at sunset. Grab a beer at the bar, followed by a quick shower and then head back to the bar for fresh sushi, ceviche and snacks. Commence telling lies about the size of the fish you caught today. Fun!

Circle Hooks

Everybody's raving about circle **hooks** just as they might about a new dance in town. The fact is, even though they don't look as if they would work very well, they work great. Hookup ratios are high and, once hooked, it's hard for a fish to throw a circle hook. The best part is that they are quite easy to remove for a quick release once the fish has been brought to the boat.

Sunday

Fish a short day inshore for roosterfish and snapper. In the afternoon, get a ride back through the mangroves to Pedregal and the airport at David for a flight back to Panama City. What a great weekend!

A WONDERFUL WEEK IN THE GULF OF CHIRIQUÍ

Beaches, whales and 5-star dining combine nicely at luxury resort Islas Secas. Billfish and whales swarm in the Gulf. **Coiba National Park** protects the best scuba diving in the country. Fishing for billfish, tuna, dorado and wahoo is unusually good. For the young and the young at heart, surfing is world-class.

RECOMMENDED PLAN: Fly directly from Panama City to the short jungle strip on remote **Islas Secas** for a week of pampered luxury in Robinson Crusoe surroundings. Prepare yourself for relaxing on the beach, under the palm trees, in a hammock, in your Pacific yurt or floating in the sea. Watch, and perhaps swim with, whales, scuba, fish, paddle around quiet tropical lagoons, explore steamy jungles and end the day indulging in truly fine dining prepared by a top chef in your remote island paradise. Have fine wines and exotic snacks delivered to your secluded yurt for greedy, gluttonous, afternoon bacchanals. Very romantic.

There are several great things to do in the area. All involve the teeming waters in and around **Coiba National Park** and **Gulf of Chiriquí National Marine Park.**

The Gulf is not particularly easy to get to. The coast is mostly lined with mangroves and there are few towns or villages. You have to fly either directly to Islas Secas Resort or to David, and then take an hour-long boat ride to get to the good stuff. It is possible to drive to beaches and a few of the more remote mangrove-surrounded villages, but you still need a boat to get to where the action is.

The Gulf's fecundity is partly due to an offshore ridge that interrupts the northward flow of extremely cold, deep currents creating a rich brew of plankton and good things for big fish to eat. Whales and pelagic fish love it. The ocean teems with life. Birds in the millions attack schools of baitfish in the zillions. Tuna, dolphins and other predatory fish species gorge in huge schools.

Don't Miss ...

- Scuba Diving Around Isla Coiba – Dive with whales, manta rays and pelagics.
- Whale Watching in the Gulf – Sperm, humpback and other beauties await your viewing pleasure.
- Fishing for Billfish Around Montuoso – Enjoy world-class fishing for marlin and sails.
- Lazing Around the Beach – Umbrella drinks, light music and sunscreen.
- Honk Down Fabulous Seafood – Eat what you catch for the freshest seafood.

Islas Secas

To get yourself right out in the middle of this rich marine environment, it's hard to beat Islas Secas. The small group of islands is a true **tropical paradise.** The surf breaks hard on the rocks of the seaward side and gentle waves lap sand beaches on the lee sides of the islands.

Islas Secas Resort is perfect if your interests are scuba diving, snorkeling, fishing, kayaking, whale watching, surfing or just lying about under the palm trees sipping umbrella drinks.

You can fly directly from Panama City to this remote paradise and land at their private, jungle airstrip. See *Best Sleeps & Eats* chapter for more information.

Where to Fish?

Local captains say that legendary fishing hot spot Hannibal Bank gets all the press, but Montuoso is where they catch all the fish. Could be.

Whales disport themselves with abandon in unusual numbers in the Gulf waters. Mostly **humpback whales** are seen, although sperm and occasionally blue whales are spotted. There really is a lot of whale activity in the area. I've seen them every time I've been on the water here, and have found myself in the water several times snorkeling or scuba diving when whales decided to come for a visit. Whale researchers (based at Islas Secas Resort) believe the whales use the area for breeding and raising their young. Humpbacks, **sperm** and **false killer whales** abound. The best way to see them is to stay at Islas Secas Resort or on Coiba Island and take small boats out exploring for them.

Fishing around Islas Secas is unusually good. Close in, roosterfish, snapper, tuna, grouper and dozens of other species are easy to catch trolling or casting to rocks and submerged ledges. The scenery is spectacular while you fish.

The lodge has several **kayaks** for guests to use. I've spent hours and hours paddling around the bay in front of the lodge and around the nearby islands, enjoying the blue of the sea and contrasting tropical greenery.

The Gulf of Chiriquí boasts a couple of the **top surfing spots** in the world. From Punta Burica, near the border with Costa Rica, to Coiba Island there are dozens of hot spots, but the ones most surfers go on about are Las Lajas and Morro Negrito.

Islas Secas staff are keen surfers themselves and love it when guests request a surf trip. They'll take you to nearby **Morro Negrito** for as long as you like and show you how it's done, if you need to learn. This is a fun trip even if you don't surf.

The wild islands in the gulf are **nesting sites for pelagic birds**. Birders will appreciate brown boobies, sandwich terns, magnificent frigate birds, and anhingas.

Guests are housed in six *casitas* (small houses – see one of them in the above photo). These are Pacific yurts, which are largish, round structures with screened windows all around. All of the casitas are situated waaaay out by themselves on top of small promontories with fabulous views out over the Pacific. It's very quiet, very casual. I spent my whole stay in the same pair of swimming trunks, only adding a T-shirt and flip-flops for meals.

If you want to go on a picnic and hang around at a remote, white-sand beach, they'll pack your lunch and drop you off where absolutely no one else is around. You can take off your clothes and run around naked—no problem. Islas Secas gives you the option of being all alone, but pampered if you like.

Mangroves

Mangroves are an amazing family of trees that grow on saltwater shorelines, their roots in the tidal water. A mangrove swamp is a unique ecosystem. The underwater forest of their roots makes a perfect habitat for barnacles, oysters, sponges, and sea squirts, which filter their food from the water as the tide goes in and out. Adolescent fish (including snook, snapper, shark, sea trout, tarpon and bonefish), shrimp, lobsters and many other creatures find shelter and food among the mangrove roots. Birds and monkeys live in the trees. Mangrove wetlands have ecological benefits too: preventing coastal erosion, filtering out pollutants, and absorbing some of the wave energy of storm surges caused by hurricanes.

The food is truly gourmet quality. The chef, Alexander Rojas, is considered to be one of the top two or three chefs in the country.

Coiba

The best diving in Panama is found in the waters in the Gulf of Chiriquí, Particularly in the **Gulf of Chiriquí National Marine Park** and around **Coiba National Park**. Diving in the Central American Pacific does not involve extensive coral reefs and crystal clear water such as one can encounter in the Caribbean. The water is so chock full of plankton that visibility is relatively low, but the rich soup means incredibly rich sea life. Fish are all over the place.

Due to nearby deep water and plenty of food to eat, divers can expect to see **deep-water pelagics** like tuna, amberjack and possibly sailfish or marlin. Huge manta rays follow divers about like dogs wanting to play. A variety of whales use the Gulf for breeding and raising their young. On a recent dive near **Coiba Island Marine Park**, a small humpback swam directly under me and turned its head for a look at me. Cool!

The Gulf around Coiba, Panama's largest island, is fringed with miles and miles of mangroves making a home for several wading bird species. Expect to see black-bellied whistling duck, roseate spoonbill, black-hooded antshrike and tropical peewee. On Coiba itself, bird species of interest include the endemic Coiba spinetail, brown-backed dove and numerous scarlet macaws.

The Gulf of Chiriquí is simply stuffed with whales. Every time I have been on the water there I have seen whales breaching, doing head stands and generally disporting themselves aggressively for tourists. While walking on trails or beaches on the islands, I always try to keep an eye on the sea for whales frolicking around.

Boca Brava

Boca Chica and Boca Brava form one mouth of a complicated system of mangrove estuaries that makes up the largest area of mangroves in Central America. **Gulf of Chiriquí National Marine Park** covers several islands, which are nesting sites for pelagic seabirds. Massive rocky headlands meeting crashing surf with Volcán Barú in the background make for spectacular scenery.

Some of the best fishing in the world is provided at comfortable **Panama Big Game Sport Fishing Club**. They specialize in taking anglers offshore for marlin and sailfish. Less famous than offshore **Hannibal Bank**, but perhaps more productive, are Isla Montuoso and Islas Ladrones. **Sailfish**, **marlin**, **dorado**, **yellow fin tuna**, huge **snapper** and **wahoo** are the local targets.

I was lucky enough to spend four days on the water at Panama Big Game this September. Wahoo to 50 lbs. were everywhere. I lost count early on. Wahoo were so numerous we declared them to be a menace. Small yellow fin tuna were hitting on top water—exciting action! Lots of small dorado, yellow snapper, blue jack, bonito, and rainbow runners kept the boys busy, with too many jack and houndfish to keep track of. Oh yeah, we ran into a couple of marlin too.

We fished four full days with Captain Tati and mate Eddie in a 31' Bertram. Most of the time we fished near pinnacles in the area of **Montuoso** but also visited **Islas Secas** for roosterfish and **Los Ladrones** for snapper. We hardly had time to fish for marlin with all the wahoo action. "No more wahoo!" was the final decision.

This cleared the decks for serious marlin battles. Early on day three, we arrived at Montuoso, quickly landed five bonito for bait and dropped them over with a couple of live blue runners for variety. Joe hooked up with a marlin almost immediately, fought for about 45 minutes and released a black weighing in the 350 lbs. neighborhood. We had barely recovered when Ron hooked another black. After about a half hour fighting the marlin in the pouring rain, Ron released his black, also running about 350 lbs.

We spent the rest of the day bottom bumping for huge snapper and casting surface plugs for tuna. Not bad for the off-season. Check out the picture of Joe with his Rooster, below. We usually arrived back at the lodge by 5:30-6:00pm, showered and spent the rest of the evening gorging on Lee's sushi, ceviche, home cooking, drinking rum and telling lies. Great fun!

8. THE CENTRAL HIGHLANDS

Thousands of retirees from North America and Europe find Boquete and the beautiful surrounding highlands to be their end-of-the-road nirvana. They tend to bring the pot of gold with them when they come, boosting the local economy. The cloud forests of El Valle attract bird watchers and Panamanians wanting to get out of the big City for the weekend. Activities include visiting coffee *fincas*, whitewater rafting and hiking the slopes of Volcán Barú (*see photo below*). The beachfront Royal Decameron offers mass-tourism all-inclusive pleasures in perhaps the most popular resort destination in Panama.

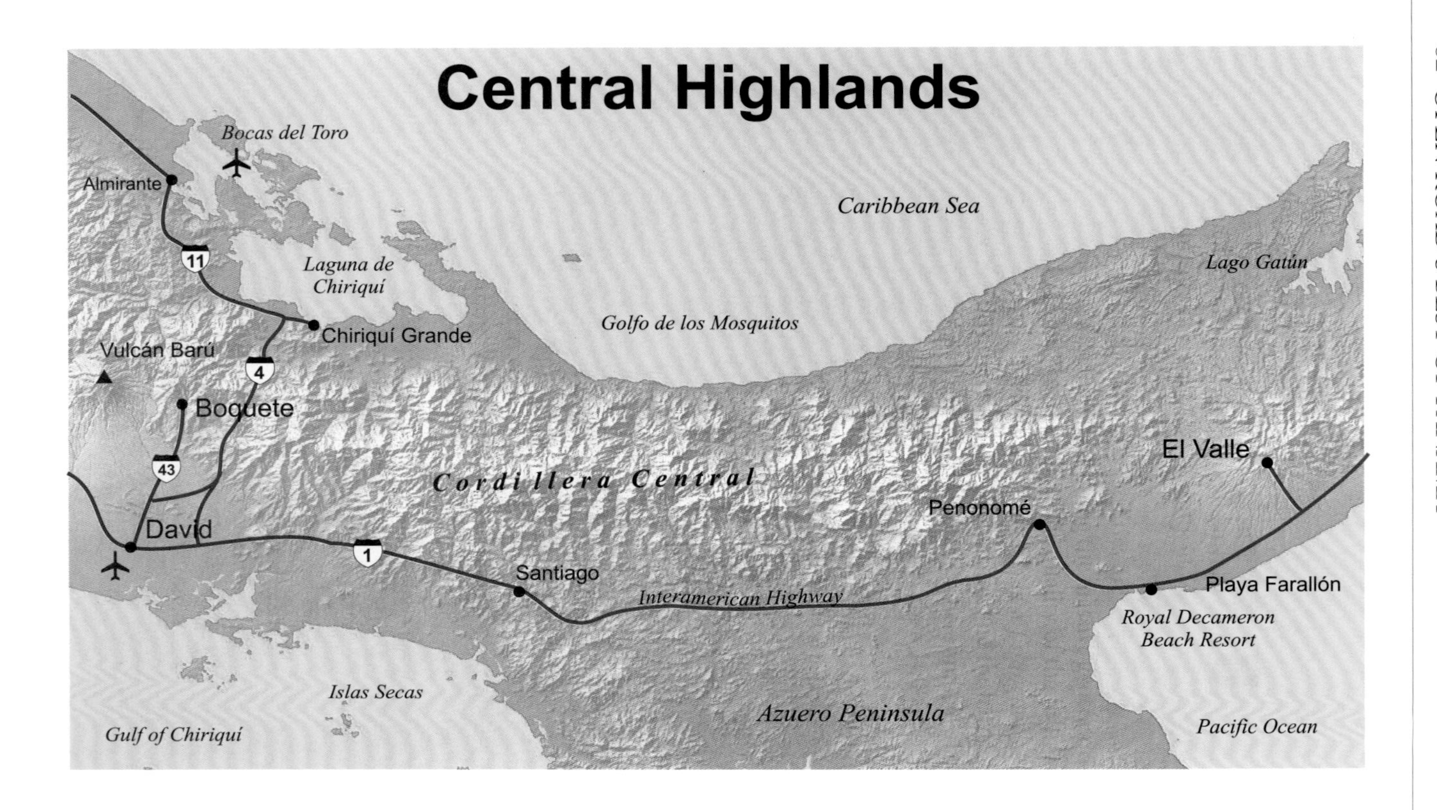
Central Highlands
Bocas del Toro
Almirante
Caribbean Sea
11
Laguna de
Chiriquí
Lago Gatún
Golfo de los Mosquitos
Chiriquí Grande
Vulcán Barú
4
Boquete
El Valle
43
Cordillera Central
Penonomé
David
1
Santiago
Playa Farallón
Interamerican Highway
Royal Decameron
Beach Resort
Islas Secas
Azuero Peninsula
Gulf of Chiriquí
Pacific Ocean

A FANTASTIC BOQUETE WEEKEND

The delights of Boquete and surroundings are many. Consume coffee and learn about its production. Hike in the surrounding cloud forests with an eye out for the resplendent quetzal. If you have energy, try white-water rafting on untamed jungle rivers. Enjoy truly fine dining at the end of the day. What a weekend!

Friday Evening

When you arrive in Boquete, check into the spanking clean and elegant **Coffee Estate Inn**. The small mountainside inn is set on 6 acres of carefully tended tropical plantings and hundreds of coffee trees (*see photo below*) high above Boquete, with fabulous views of the mountains and valley.

The Canadian owners have a passion for **fine coffee**, and grow several varieties of *típica*, heirloom and modern hybrid beans. They roast their beans on site and make their fabulous coffee available to guests. I enjoyed a wonderful educational stroll through their grounds with owner Barry. He spent several hours telling me about growing and preparing coffee beans, and about the coffee business in general. Fascinating!

If you are unsure of how to proceed to get the most out of your short stay in the area, call Barry and his wife Jane ahead of time and they can help you plan a leisurely itinerary and arrange for transportation, guides, or whatever.

There are several interesting restaurants in the area, but the best food in the entire province is provided in the Coffee Estate Inn's dining room. Dinner is prepared on special request so be sure to make the request in advance. The food is wonderful. Even though she only cooks on a small scale, mostly for her own guests, Jane is one of the best chefs in the country. The Inn's reputation for fine dinners is well deserved.

Saturday

Wildlife, coffee and retirement are what many visitors to Boquete come for. Start the day with a visit to **Café Ruiz**. Their tour encompasses the farm itself, the drying process at the *beneficio,* a visit to the roaster and, of course, the all-important part of any coffee farm tour—the cupping (drinking the stuff). It's a nice tour and a good opportunity to learn about, sample and buy local coffees.

> **ALTERNATE PLAN**
> Check into the beachfront Royal Decameron, perhaps the most popular resort destination in Panama, and indulge shamelessly in demolishing enormous buffets, lying around uselessly on the beach and clogging up the dance floor in the disco at night. This is reasonably well done, mass-market tourism. It's nothing to be ashamed of—we've all done it before.

The mountainous, jungle-covered central spine of Panama gives rise to a number of world-class **rafting** rivers. The **Chiriquí Viejo**, **Rió Grande** and **Chagres** Rivers offer everything from quiet floats to class IV and V rapids. Outfitters haul tourists in vans to put-in sites, usually a couple of hours away from Boquete. Aventuras Panamá offers several different trips for different levels of rafters.

Sunday

An early start is best for **birding**. Boquete has a population of dedicated and knowledgeable bird guides. Hans van der Voorens is a good choice. He is well equipped, knows the area well and has an encyclopedic knowledge of tropical birds.

Nearby **Barú Volcano Park** is one of the favorite areas for bird expeditions. Quetzals, trogons and three-wattled bellbirds are prime targets for birdwatchers. This is probably the best area in the world to find quetzals.

A FANTASTIC EL VALLE WEEKEND

The beauty of El Valle attracts an upscale crowd of retired gringos and well-heeled Latinos from all over the world. The beautiful mountain valleys and nearby cloud forests are home to an amazing variety of wildlife. Flocks of birders make pilgrimages to the area for glimpses of resplendent quetzals and three-wattled bellbirds.

Friday Evening

It's an easy three-hour drive from Panama City, along the coast and up into the mountains, to El Valle. Be ready for much cooler weather. Temperatures in the 70s are not unusual and there is an inordinate amount of rain. When it's not raining it's misting, so be ready with your hat and raingear. The weather is all part of the fun. The rain forest, after all, is the main attraction here.

I don't see any point in staying anywhere other than the wonderful **Canopy Lodge**. It's a major birding lodge in the middle of one of the most picturesque valleys in the highlands. The 150-acre grounds of the lodge itself teem with birds and exotic flowers.

Saturday

Get up quite early to take advantage of the wonderful birding conditions. The lodge has two of the very best bird guides in the country on hand. No birder, I spent a morning with guide **Faustino Sanchez** (Tino) just strolling around the grounds and on nearby trails, and spotted over one hundred species. Remarkable!

The knowledgeable guides and tour leaders show films and give educational lectures on rainy afternoons. Hardcore twitchers ignore the rain and go birding anyway.

After a wonderful lunch back at the lodge, you can simply walk a quarter mile to the famous zip line attraction **Canopy Adventure**. For $40 you get to zip through the jungle and over waterfalls over 100 feet up in the air. The runs are not particularly steep. The area is perfect for wildlife viewing, especially birds, after everyone stops screaming from the zip line adrenaline rush.

You can spend the afternoon here zipping, observing wildlife and soaking in the ice-cold forest stream. It's a beautiful place.

In the evening, the lodge lays on a great buffet and the wine starts to flow. I enjoy these meals when I can meet and talk with interesting travelers about their trips around the world. After dinner, serious birders spend hours discussing and cataloguing their finds from hikes on nearby trails.

Sunday

I'm up for yet another morning of chasing LBBs (Little Brown Birds) and their show biz relations: **quetzals**, **trogons** (*see photo on previous page*) and **three-wattled bellbirds.** One of the top birding tours in Panama takes in **Altos de Maria**, a new, gigantic housing development that has plenty of open area alongside almost virgin forest allowing unusual viewing opportunities. Expect to encounter purplish-backed quail-doves, purple-throated trogons, brown-billed scythebills and, of course, black-crowned antpittas.

Any excuse to get out into the wonders of the forest is a good excuse, and observing LBBs works for me.

A WONDERFUL WEEK IN BOQUETE & EL VALLE

A week is time enough to sample the three best areas in the region: a few days in the Boquete area sampling coffee, whitewater rafting and fine dining; a few days twitching in El Valle; a few days soaking up some sun/sand on the beach.

RECOMMENDED PLAN: Spend a couple of nights in Boquete enjoying fresh-roasted mountain coffee, the spectacular scenery of Volcán Barú and whitewater rafting. In El Valle, check into birding paradise **Canopy Lodge** and hunt down the resplendent quetzal and three-wattled bellbird. Finish off the week luxuriating on the beach and gorging on high school cafeteria food at the all-inclusive **Royal Decameron**.

Boquete

The Canadian owners of the **Coffee Estate Inn** have a passion for fine coffee, and grow several varieties of *típica*, heirloom and modern hybrid beans. They roast their beans on site and make their fabulous coffee available to guests. Spanking clean and elegant, the small mountainside inn is set in 6 acres of carefully tended tropical plantings and hundreds of coffee trees.

Many guests fly into the country and come straight to Barry and Jane, who are very familiar with the country and help their guests plan their time and make arrangements for their in-country travel.

Several good restaurants have sprung up to serve the flood of gringo visitors and residents. **Machu Picchu** is a Peruvian favorite with a large menu heavy on seafood. **El Zaranya** is a Lebanese restaurant with all the expected pita, humus, baba ghanoush, sambusek, estifas and skewered meats with rice. **Deli Barú** is a great deli with all the expected meats, cheeses, pickles, breads and interesting bottled drinks. They do up great sandwiches. Yet another Peruvian spot, Delicias del Peru, specializes in *Ceviche Peruviana* and fried ceviche.

Don't Miss ...

- **Coffee** – Find out why so many people rate Panamanian coffee tops.
- **Volcán Barú** – Marvel at the cloud forest–covered slopes of the dead cone.
- **Bird Watching** – The last one to see a resplendent quetzal has to buy the drinks.
- **Retirement Properties** – Even if you don't plan on buying anything, everyone expects you to shop for real estate anyway.

But the best table in town is at the Coffee Estate Inn. Dinner is prepared on special request, usually just for guests, so be sure to call well ahead. The food is wonderful. Even though she only cooks on a small scale, mostly for her own guests, Jane is one of the best chefs in the country. The Inn's reputation for fine dinners is well deserved. Gourmands drive from Panama City just for her dinners. You're definitely going to eat well while visiting Boquete.

Shopping is not really part of the Boquete experience. Although there are a variety of tourist-oriented items for sale, the only thing really worth purchasing while you are in the area is wonderful Panamanian coffee. Boquete in particular is a famous coffee-producing region. Some of the best and most expensive coffees in the world are produced on the slopes of Volcán Barú.

Café Ruiz has a roadside shop featuring their own, locally-produced products, and is the starting and ending point for the company's tour of their nearby farm, *beneficio* and roasting operation. Wonderful, fresh roasted coffee is for sale for immediate consumption or for the road. Various roasts are available as well as examples of some of the more interesting local heirloom *típico* varieties. Ask for some **geisha**, currently the trendiest of coffee varieties.

This is not an area for nightlife, other than a decent **casino** in David. Observing wildlife, drinking coffee, retiring and hiking are what most visitors do. Most go to bed early to be ready for the 6am bird walk.

With nearby **Volcán Barú**, mountain hiking simply doesn't get much better. A number of ancient Indian trails are still serviceable and are still in use by local Indians. **Quetzal** searches in the cloud forest are popular. This very colorful, fancy-feathered bird is the end-all and be-all for many birders.

Guides Hans & Terry van der Vooren lead groups on a variety of highland tours including bird trips, coffee farm visits and trips to see a **Ngöbe Buglé Indian village**. They lead groups in English, Spanish, Dutch and German.

Soaking Wet?

Rafting is guaranteed to get you soaking wet. That's okay. Outfitters will carry your dry stuff in sealed, waterproof bags. Wear shorts and a T-shirt, with sandals or tennis shoes. If you bring a camera, make sure it's waterproof!

White-water rafting enthusiasts come from around the world to challenge themselves on the Chiriquí Viejo, Rió Grande and Chagres Rivers, which offer everything from quiet floats to **class IV and V rapids**. Outfitters haul punters in vans to put in sites, usually a couple of hours away from lodging. Aventuras Panamá, Tel. 507-260-0044, has several different trips for different levels of rafters.

El Valle

Birders flock to El Valle to view the largest concentration of resplendent quetzals anywhere in the world, and count on adding significantly to their life lists during visits to **Canopy Lodge**, Los Altos de Maria and other **twitching** (birding) **hot spots**.

Canopy Lodge is a major birding lodge in the middle of one of the most picturesque valleys in the highlands. The 150-acre grounds of the lodge itself teem with birds and exotic flowers. A babbling stream runs through the place, almost but not quite drowning out the sounds of hundreds of birds that fill the grounds.

Serious birders spend hours after dinner discussing and cataloguing their finds from hikes on nearby trails. The lodge has two of the very **best bird guides** in the country on hand. Guests usually combine a visit

here with a visit to their sister lodge, Canopy Tower just outside Panama City, to round out their Panamanian bird watching experience. The lodge is almost a secret. There is no sign on the road in front and it is not heavily marketed. In spite of this almost-anonymity, the lodge is usually full of serious birders from around the world. Many guests I met had made multiple trips to birding meccas like Ecuador, Brazil and Peru. The knowledgeable guides and tour leaders show films and give educational lectures on rainy afternoons. Hard core twitchers ignore the rain and go birding anyway.

For the adventurous, for $40, you get to zip through the jungle and over waterfalls over 100 feet up n the air at wonderful **Canopy Adventure**. This is a large area of protected forest, rich with wildlife, with a touristy zip line running through it. The runs are not particularly steep. The area is perfect for viewing wildlife, especially birds, after everyone stops screaming from the zip line adrenaline rush. They are located just up the road from Canopy Lodge.

What is a Cloud Forest?

When moisture-filled warm air blows in from the ocean to meet the barrier of a high mountain range, it condenses to form a standing mass of clouds. The 100% humidity and nearly constant rain support an incredibly lush flora. Visitors see a thick forest mysteriously shrouded in fog, with damp-loving lichens and mosses covering every square inch of available space. Trees are draped with epiphytes (plants that grow in trees, such as bromeliads and orchids), creating an entire ecosystem high in the forest canopy. Many species of animals spend their entire lives up here, and you won't see them from the ground.

One of the top birding tours in Panama takes in **Altos de Maria**, a new, gigantic housing development that has plenty of open area alongside almost virgin forest, allowing unusual viewing opportunities. Expect to encounter purplish-backed quail-doves, purple-throated trogons, brown-billed scythebills and, of course, black-crowned antpittas.

Decameron

About four hours outside Panama City, on a sparkling sand beach, sits the **Royal Decameron**, perhaps the most famous place to stay in Panama. The all-inclusive, **beachfront** Decameron is (and this is a puzzle to me) one of the most popular destinations in the country. Everything is included: meals, drinks, water sports toys, even cigarettes. Simply hold up your hand with fingers set in the classic smoker's "V" and, magically, a cigarette will appear in it. No extra charge. It's like a cruise ship on land. This is mass tourism but reasonably well done.

The beach is quite a nice one, long and sandy. Local seafood shacks and drink stands can be found at a nearby small village. There are several pools and a variety of resort sports available. Rooms are reasonably comfortable with air-conditioning and all the usual goodies expected in a three star place. They have a spa and a casino.

9. DARIEN

The notorious Darien Gap is still notorious and still a gap, a vast region of rarely visited jungle-covered mountains and impenetrable swamps. It's one of the last unspoiled tropical forests in the world and a great place to visit in spite of the difficulties of traveling there. The best way to see the area is to place yourself in the competent hands of Ancon Expeditions – www.anconexpeditions.com – who maintain their own jungle lodges and operate charter flights to remote jungle clearings. If you're hard-core, they'll guide you on a 14-day cross-isthmus Darien trek on foot and by canoe.

On the Pacific coast of Darien, at the mountainous edge of wild, impenetrable jungle, Tropic Star Lodge luxuriously treats guests to the best sport fishing for billfish in the world on offshore Zane Grey Reef.

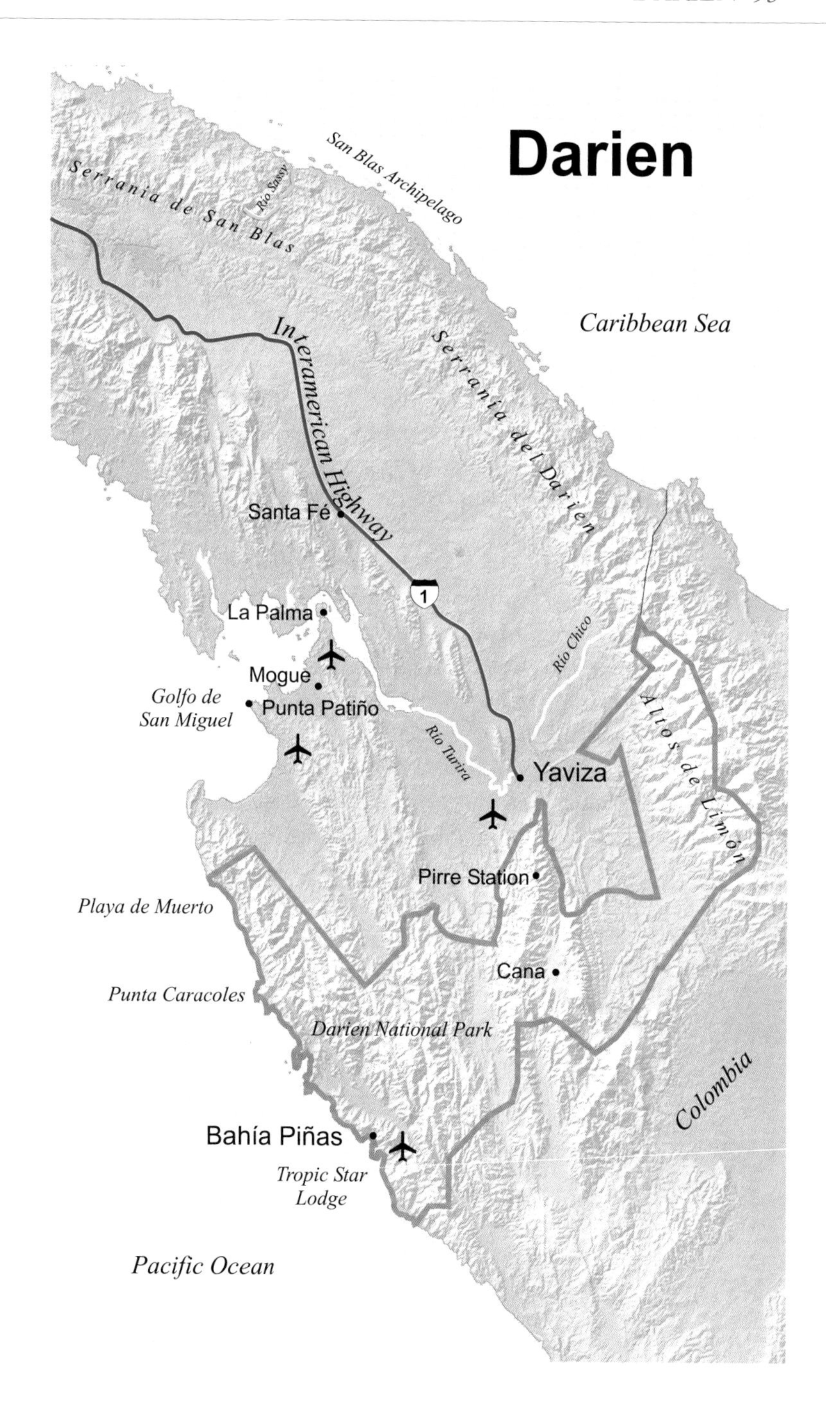
Darien
San Blas Archipelago
Serrania de San Blas
Rio Sassy
Caribbean Sea
Interamerican Highway
Serrania del Darien
Santa Fé
1
La Palma
Rio Chico
Mogue
Golfo de
San Miguel
Punta Patiño
Altos de Limón
Rio Turira
Yaviza
Pirre Station
Playa de Muerto
Cana
Punta Caracoles
Darien National Park
Colombia
Bahía Piñas
Tropic Star
Lodge
Pacific Ocean

A FANTASTIC DARIEN WEEKEND

Darien is not an easy place to explore. There are almost no roads—most of it is still primary and secondary tropical rain forest. You can explore the area in two ways: fly into jungle airstrips to remote lodges for birding and wildlife viewing, or fly along the Pacific coast almost to the border with Columbia to fish at the luxurious Tropic Star Lodge. Both involve charter flights and going with an organized group.

Ancon Expeditions operates the only accommodations in remote areas of Darien. Fortunately, they do a great job running their jungle lodges and wildlife tours.

Friday

Traveling with Ancon Expeditions is an easy way to see the primitive areas of Darien up close in just a couple of days and still be relatively comfortable. Transportation is provided from Panama City area hotels to Albrook airport for the flight to La Palma in Darien at the mouth of the Tuira River. The trip by boat to Ancon's lodge in the 65,000-acre **Punta Patiño Nature Reserve** takes about an hour.

After lunch at the lodge, hike the Piedra Candela trail through tropical dry forest to the beach. You can then hang around the beach for the usually spectacular sunset or head back to the lodge for cocktail hour and a group-style dinner. In the evening, take a short walk to the **wetlands** to see **capybaras**, **caimans** and **owls**.

Saturday

Head up the **Mogue River** by motorized dugout to visit the **Embera Indians.** This is a moderately staged interaction. The village is real enough, but the villagers have obviously done this before and follow the script. Numerous handicrafts and such will be presented for sale. In spite of the uncomfortable nature of all such encounters between affluent First Worlders and fairly authentic, indigenous jungle dwellers, the trip is worthwhile. You get to learn about how such people live and they get to marvel at our strange ways and earn a couple of bucks.

The trip up and back is a **great birding** and wildlife observation opportunity. **Roseate spoonbill, ibis, osprey** and **raccoons** are common and, on the return coastal tour of the reserve, you can inspect the sea bird nesting areas of El Morro.

The remaining part of the day is open for exploring near the lodge or soaking up hammock time. I enjoy dinners with the other guests in the evening. Invariably, I meet interesting travelers with great stories about their exploits in other parts of Panama and other countries.

Sunday

The best part of the day is the boat ride through the bay back to La Palma for the trip back to Panama City. **Dolphins** and even **whales** are commonly seen.

A FANTASTIC TROPIC STAR WEEKEND

Tropic Star at Bahía Piñas is all about big-time sport fishing. Wealthy anglers come from around the world to rub shoulders in the lodge at night after fishing with international business executives, celebrities and fish-loving playboys. The luxury lodge is home to more world records than any other place on the planet.

Friday

Take the included transport from your Panama City hotel to the VIP lounge at Albrook for your charter flight to **Bahía Piñas** and Tropic Star Lodge. The basic airstrip is near a small village of about 150 people (75 of them police). A tractor-pulled cart transports guests to a small river

where a launch awaits to take guests on a 10-minute ride around the point to the lodge. Of course, a large cooler full of beer and soft drinks accompanies all of this transportation action.

Once at the lodge, a little orientation talk and lunch is followed by an afternoon **fishing inshore** for wahoo, roosterfish, snapper, grouper and other tropical lovelies. Fishing is done on lovingly restored **1957 Bertram 31s**. I've fished *much* newer boats that were in *much* worse condition. The lodge takes immaculate care of everything. This is a first-class operation all the way around.

Drinks in the bar after fishing are accompanied by deep-fried fish fingers made from just-caught fish and homemade, hot potato chips. Hard to beat. The food is very well prepared and presented. Service is spot on and friendly. Expect very fresh dorado, tuna, wahoo ceviche, and main courses with interesting sauces.

Saturday

Early in the morning, coffee appears at your door on a tray. After a full hot breakfast, head to the dock for a full day of fishing for marlin, sails and tuna. I've **caught billfish every day** I've fished here. I suppose it's possible to get skunked but I didn't hear of it happening the times I've been there.

It's a long day out at sea hauling in huge fish, so bring a good hat and sunscreen. Just about everything else will be provided.

Sunday

You'll get up at a reasonable hour, enjoy a wonderful breakfast in the lounge, and then head back to Bahía Piñas for the short charter flight back to Panama City. Be sure to get a window seat for the spectacular views of the Islas Perlas as you fly over.

A WONDERFUL WEEK IN DARIEN

A week is time enough to go to one of the **remote lodges** operated by Ancon Expeditions to observe harpy eagles, and still have plenty of time for a few days far down on the Pacific coast in "*National Geographic* country" fishing for billfish, dorado, tuna and wahoo.

RECOMMENDED PLAN: Be sure to stay at one of Ancon Expedition's remote jungle lodges. **Cana** and **Punta Patiño** offer chances to stay in reasonable comfort waaay out in the middle of the jungle. If you are an angler, **Tropic Star Lodge** at Bahía Piñas is universally regarded as the top billfish lodge in the world. Fly in for a few days of fast fishing exploits.

Cana

Cana Field Station, surrounded by **Darien National Park,** is one of the top birding destinations in the world. **Ancon Expeditions** organizes trips to Cana, provides rustic accommodations (hot showers) and top guides. Trips to Cana are either five or eight days long and are always accompanied by a top naturalist guide. Visitors are flown into the **remote airstrip** on charter flights.

Operated by Ancon Expeditions of Panama and reachable only by charter flight, the lodge consists of not much more than 8 double cabins, a dining hall with observation deck and two bathrooms. Sounds dreadful but it's not. There is hot water and the food is good. The area is regarded as one of the **top two or three birding sites in the world**. Birders and serious outdoor enthusiasts make up almost all of the guests.

Ancon arranges 5- and 8-day trips accompanied by one of their naturalist/guides. If you are the outdoorsy type, you will love the place. There's not much there except for a system of trails into the surrounding mountainous jungle. The hard core among the guests can spend a night

Don't Miss ...

- Visiting the Embera Indians
- Birding and looking for the big wild cats in area parks and reserves
- Fishing for the big ones in the waters off Tropic Star Lodge

or two high in the cloud forest at the **Pirri Tent Camp**. This is the trip of a lifetime.

Punta Patiño Nature Reserve

The most famous of the feathered inhabitants of Darien is the **harpy eagle** (*see photo below*). This mighty bird is known to jump down and haul off monkeys, sloths and other small furry creatures to devour in their nests at leisure. Hard-core birders hope to view them on their nest with the young ones **tearing dead things into shreds** and swallowing them. Quite a show. Punta Patiño Nature Reserve is the place to see them.

Punta Patiño is on the Pacific coast, so you are exposed to **both lowland and upland species**. The lodging is perhaps a little more comfortable than Cana. You have hot water and private baths. Food is served family-style in the large dining room with spectacular views out to sea and over the jungled hills. This is harpy eagle country and birders flock here to observe them in their nests.

White-nosed **coatis** (locally known as *pizotes*) are frequently seen, and they are friendly and fun. **Monkeys** are everyone's favorites, and they are pretty common (a little too common, say the owners of stolen sunglasses and hats). Panama has seven species of monkeys: black-handed spider, white-faced capuchins, Geoffrey's tamarins, rufous-naped tamarins, night (owl) monkeys, squirrel and mantled howler monkeys, whose cries boom through the forest.

We'd all love to see a **wild cat**, and Panama has six species: jaguar, oncilla , ocelot, puma, margay (*see photo in sidebar*) and jaguarundis. Outside of a zoo or rehabilitation center, however, you're unlikely to spot one of these secretive, nocturnal predators.

The only way to get here is with a trip organized by the efficient Ancon Expeditions. Their Punta Patiño Lodge is located on a bluff overlooking the Pacific with **hundreds of square miles of primary and secondary tropical forest** behind. Guests can explore a varied set of marine and coastal environments with nearby wetlands, rivers and **Embera Indian communities**. Ancon's guides are some of the best trained anywhere. Birders who come here from around the world are sure to add significantly to their life lists.

Observing the Animals

The greatest thrill in Panama is the chance to see wild animals going about their daily business in the forest. If you spend some time in one or more of the parks and preserves, your chances of seeing some critters are good. However, some animals are much more easily seen than others, and some visitors have unrealistic expectations.

If you really want to see some of the rarer forest denizens, visit a remote park, walk quietly, and **take your hikes in the early morning or just before dusk.** I highly recommend hiring a local guide, who can show you animals (and plants) that you would never see on your own.

Better than rustic, the 10 cabins are air-conditioned and quite comfortable. All have private bathrooms. The dining hall serves up groaning buffets of wonderful food.

Bahía Piñas

Although the Darien area is famous for **impenetrable jungles** and **fetid swamps**, it also happens to have what is without doubt the **top fishing lodge in the world. Tropic Star Lodge** hosts up to 35 anglers in true luxury. Fine dining, air-conditioned rooms, true top-shelf service are difficult to accomplish miles from anywhere in *National Geographic* country, but Tropic Star manages. Everything is brought in from Panama City by plane or supply boat. Fishing is done on immaculately maintained, classic **31' Bertrams.** Captains and mates train for years or even decades to earn their coveted positions.

The fishing action takes place about 20 miles offshore where cold Southern currents meet undersea mountains, causing plankton-rich upwellings. This attracts small fish by the billions, which attracts big game fish like **marlin and tuna in the millions.**

I have fished at the top fishing lodges in Central America and the Caribbean, and can confidently say that Tropic Star offers the **best fishing for billfish** and other tropical species. The lodge is almost always full. You need to book as much as a year in advance to be sure of having a place.

Anglers at Tropic Star aim primarily at billfish. Black, blue and striped marlin are reliable and multiple sailfish hookups are common. You can't beat a by catch of dorado, tuna, wahoo, roosterfish and seemingly zillions of other tropic game and table fish.

Birders who visit the Bahía Piñas area can expect to see great green macaws, tody motmots and puffbirds. White-fronted nunbirds are the stars in the region. If you go offshore, **magnificent pelagics** perform their acrobatics for you. Expect to see brown boobies, brown noddys, wedge-rumped storm petrels. Tropic Star Lodge has **naturalist guides** and forest rangers but no trained bird guides.

A stay at Tropic Star is not cheap. The facilities are top-quality and deep-sea fishing uses a lot of fuel. So do running the massive generators and hauling supplies in from Panama City. The quality of the fishing makes the price seem small. Understand that this is a *fishing* lodge.

There's not much else to do other than fish. Celebrities and the hardest of the hard-core anglers from all over the world come here and pay the price. Book well in advance since they rarely are less than 100% full.

See *Best Activities* for more information about fishing at Tropic Star.

10. PANAMA IN TWO WEEKS

With two weeks, you will have time to visit the majority of Panama's attractions. Inevitably, you'll realize you want to come back for more. For more details on activities, hotels, and restaurants, see the *Best Activities* and *Best Sleeps & Eats* chapters.

RECOMMENDED PLAN: Using **Panama City** as a hub, you'll be able to get your toes into the Caribbean sand in the **San Blas Islands** and **Bocas del Toro** and dip into the Pacific at **Bahía Piñas**. You can visit the central highlands retirement Eden, **Boquete**, and still have time to spend a few days doing some serious angling on the Pacific coast of **Darien**. Explore different layers of the **tropical rainforest canopy** at Canopy Tower. And you can spend several days in throbbing Panama City.

Day One – Panama City

Most flights to Panama from North America arrive in the afternoon at Tocumen International. Flights from Panama City to internal destinations leave from **Albrook Airport**, an hour's drive away, on the other side of the city. Most domestic flights leave in the morning or early afternoon to take advantage of the best flying conditions. There's usually not enough time to make an internal connection the same day. There is an Aeroperlas flight to Bocas del Toro at 3pm that you might just catch.

You don't have to plan on setting aside a couple of days for Panama City. You'll probably end up staying there, or in the immediate vicinity anyway to make plane connections, so youwill definitely get to see and enjoy Panama City thoroughly.

Book your Panama City hotel well in advance. In spite of the seeming plethora of hotels, all the hotels seem to be almost perpetually booked up. Do not assume you can simply pop into town and grab any hotel you want.

I suggest the comfortable **Intercontinental Miramar Panama.** It's a little on the pricey side but the location is good if you are interested in carrying on in the clubs and bars of the **Calle Uruguay** entertainment district—it starts right across the street. You can crawl back to your hotel in the wee hours after a night of salsa and mojitos. It has wonderful views of the city and the Pacific. You can watch the freighters passing in and out of the canal along the breakwater.

Don't Miss ...

- San Blas – The islands and fiercely independent Kuna Indians remain supremely photogenic.
- Tropic Star Lodge – Located in the remote Darien, this is the very best bill fishing in the world.
- Bocas del Toro – Enjoy secluded white sand beaches from your hammock. Sip umbrella drinks.
- Transit The Panama Canal – Check out the locks from the inside. Get up close to Panamax container ships.
- Birding On Pipeline Road – add significantly to your life list within minutes of your arrival. Amazing bird life!

The loaded-with-ambiance **Bristol** has a reputation as the best hotel in Panama City; it has a way to go before it lives up to the hype. Quite simply: it ain't worth the money. The Miramar Intercontinental, nearby, has nicer rooms for a little less money and great views if you don't have to have the ambiance.

If you don't like the idea of staying in a big city for even one night, there are several quiet and secluded options within a very short drive of town. **Canopy Tower** is in the middle of the rainforest and the **Intercontinental Playa Bonita** is on a secluded beach. Both are within 20 minutes of Panama City.

Now rendezvous with an English speaking driver for a guided tour of Panama City. Taxis in Panama City are cheap. Most rides are $1 to $3. You can hire almost any cab in town for $10 or so an hour, but most drivers speak only fair English, if any. Hiring a private car with English speaking driver/guide can be cheaper than renting a car with *much* less hassle. You simply have the driver meet you in front of your hotel and drop you off wherever.

After a short afternoon sightseeing and getting your bearings in Panama City, relax in your hotel room and get ready for gobbling up piles of **great seafood**, followed by an evening of enjoying live music or possibly dancing until daylight. It's all there for you if you want it.

Panama City has dozens of world-class restaurants. For fine dining, **Eurasia** is one of the top restaurants in town, especially for seafood. For beef, head to **Gaucho's**. Don't drink too much at dinner. The night is young in hot, hot, hot Panama City and you'll need some reserves of energy to see the city at night.

Panama City is famous for late night partying, dancing, live music and elegant casinos. If you can still get it up for nightlife after dining at one of places just mentioned, I suggest an evening of serious live music consumption at **Havana Rumba** on the **Amador Causeway**. Local musicians play to a mostly local crowd who are serious about listening

to keen musicians playing Latin classics. This is a very good evening out if you appreciate live music in a quiet, intimate setting.
There are 36 legal gambling **casinos** in Panama. Fancy Las Vegas style palaces (almost) compete with down-at-the-heels joints and everything in between. A few Panama City casinos, such as the **Veneto**, are magnets for interesting young women looking for interesting (and big spending) gringos. Stop in after 11pm to find out.

If you still crave more nightlife, don't worry, you'll be passing through Panama city again during your two week Panama jaunt.
In the morning, get your act together and your bags packed. If you have time before your connecting flight to Bocas del Toro, indulge in some simple sightseeing or shopping.

You could do your shopping on your last day of the trip, but that could be risky. I suggest buying molas for souvenirs and gifts. They are truly works or art, usually fairly inexpensive and lightweight for carrying back home on the plane. The best place in Panama to buy molas is not in the San Blas where the Kuna Indians make them, but at **Flory Saltzman's Molas** next to the El Panama Hotel. She and her mother have been working with the Kuna for many years and she has an enormous collection to choose from. Her prices are about the same as you would pay if you bought your molas in the San Blas.

If you find yourself in Panama City on a Saturday morning with nothing to do, go on a transit of the Panama Canal aboard a quaint launch. You could do the canal tour canal tour in morning and then fly in the afternoon on the 3pm flight to **Bocas del Toro**.

Days 2 and 3 – Bocas del Toro

At the airport in Bocas, you'll be met and transported a mile or so to the water taxi dock for a ride in a launch to your lodge.

I suggest staying at either **Al Natural** or **Garden of Eden**. Both are romantic and full of character.

The Garden of Eden is a three-rooms-around-the-pool B&B on its own little island by itself. The American hosts are from the Keys and know how to cook good seafood and enjoy the island lifestyle. It's one of my favorite places in Panama.

Al Natural is further away on a quiet sand beach. The guest casitas are set privately in the trees at the edge of the water. It's very laid back with a charismatic host and delicious group meals.

You must get into Bocas Town for at least an afternoon. Go at night if you want to party loud, long and hard. Figure out how you're going to get back to your lodge before you set out for the night. Most launches and motor taxis don't run after dark for fear of collisions with other boats (they don't tend to use running lights).

There is plenty to do in Bocas. Besides the famous pleasures of drinking and shouting, water sports are the big draw to the area. Snorkeling, surfing, fishing and kayaking are all wonderful here. Don't miss a snorkeling/beachcombing trip to Cayos Zapatillas. The small, picturesque islets are surrounded with good snorkeling.

While not a first-class scuba diving destination, Bocas has excellent snorkeling. **Parque Nacional Marino Isla Bastamientos** is a standout dive site. **Jampan Tours** offers snorkeling trips. I suggest the shorter $17 trip. The snorkeling around the national park at **Zapatilla Island** is not quite as good as on the shorter, cheaper trip to **Crawl Cay.** The *Survivor* TV series was filmed on Zapatilla, so many visitors insist on a visit. It's not that exciting.

For hard-core divers, **Bocas Water Sports** offers full PADI services. The have two and three tank dives with all the usual rental equipment.

Jampan or your lodge can arrange for trolling for tuna from local dugouts or small outboards. Most of the time anglers can expect to nail a kingfish or two, a couple of snapper and some jack or needlefish. Tarpon, snook and other interesting game fish are in the area, but the fishery has not been explored or developed for visitors to enjoy.

Jampan Tours also has a variety of houseboats and other medium-sized craft available for multi-day cruises through the archipelago. This is a great way to see the area. The boats come all set up with cooking facilities, bedding and snorkeling gear.

The Bocas del Toro Archipelago is a wonderful area for kayaking. If you can, try to arrange to paddle around the Zapatillas or Swan Cay. The water and scenery are superb. There always seems to be one more tropical isle off in the distance that needs to be explored. The water around Bocas town teems with boat traffic and fecal matter, so wakes and ear infections can be a problem. The best kayaking is far from town. Many of the lodges have kayaks for guest use.

Bocas is the **top surf destination** in Panama. There may be better waves elsewhere, but Bocas has all the other stuff surfers love: cheap eats, cheap sleeps and rowdy nightspots booming out DJ sounds. The best waves generally arrive from December through March; although nearby storms can kick things up nicely from time to time.

Red Frog Beach is perhaps the most famous spot, but **The Dumps**, **Playa Punch** and **Playa Primera** offer waves to challenge jaded surfers. You can rent surfboards in town from a small shack near the park.

Isla Escudo de Veraguas in the Bocas del Toro archipelago is the only place on the planet where you can find the tiny Escudo hummingbird.

In Panama, you'll only find the elusive stub-tailed spadebill in these islands. Three-wattled bellbirds and Montezuma oropendolas are also attractions for birders. Swan Cay, *Isla Pájaros,* hosts the only Caribbean breeding colony of the red-billed tropicbird. Nearby San San Pond Sack wetlands are a major draw for birders. Ancon Expeditions at the Bocas Inn can set you up with proper birding guides.

Parque Nacional Marino Isla Bastamientos protects large areas of Isla Bastamientos and the nearby underwater reefs. Some snorkeling spots are marked and have buoys for tying boats.

Cayos Zapatillas are cool little beach islands all by themselves with no one on them but you and your fellow tourists. These two tiny islets are picture postcard perfect with white sand and a few palm trees. This is a good spot for a picnic or romantic interlude.

There are several nice beaches in Bocas del Toro. **Playa La Cabana, Big Creek, Red Frog** and **Playa Bluff** are perhaps the best. Some are good for swimming and others for surfing. Watch out for undertow and tide rips where the surf is high.

If you simply must indulge your addiction, you can play Red Frog Beach Resort's Arnold Palmer-designed 18-holer.

Nightlife and entertainment are what Bocas Town is all about. The place heaves with loud music and the shouts of partygoers every night until past dawn. The hottest, trendiest spots change, so check with your lodge or hotel for recommendations about the newest and best place to get smashed. Two places that never seem to go out of style are **Bum Fuck's** (named after its colorful owner Bill Baumfaulk) and **Barco Hundido** (sunken ship). Getting smashed is pretty much what it's all about. Avoid watermelon *mojitos.*

Be sure you have a safe way back to your lodge after carousing in Bocas Town. Most launches don't have lights and won't run after dark due to the danger of collision with other boats that don't have lights. Okay.

In the morning, your lodge will arrange you transportation back to Bocas and get you on the right water taxi to get to the ramshackle docks at **Almirante** on the mainland where you will meet your driver for the trip over the mountains to Boquete.

Almirante is a crumbling mess, and numerous underemployed entrepreneurs hang about the docks, hoping to help a gringo like yourself with luggage, taxis, real estate, drug purchases, whatever. With luck, you can make eye contact with your waiting driver before the boat is finished tying up so you will have a guide through the awaiting, hustling hordes.

The ride over the mountains to Boquete passes through areas of agriculture and areas of thick, tropical rainforest. Keep your camera handy: the views over the valleys and out to sea on both coasts are dramatic.

Upon arrival in Boquete, check into the **Coffee Estate Inn** for the night. Be sure to arrange ahead of time for one of their delicious dinners. They usually only cook for their guests. Their elegant and famous evenings of fine dining and fine coffee (which they grow on-site) are well-known throughout Panama.

After dinner, enjoy the beauty of the valley from the deck of your room.

Day 4 - Boquete

Due to its natural beauty and cool but tropical climate, Boquete has become not just a tourism destination, but also a retirement destination for thousands of gringos from North America, Europe and South Africa. Hiking, white-water rafting, enjoying fine food and drink, and observing wildlife top the list of things to do. Boquete in particular is a famous coffee-producing region. Some of the best and

most expensive coffees in the world are produced on the slopes of Volcán Barú.

In the morning, engage a guide for a hike through nearby mountain trails. You have an excellent chance of observing the famous resplendent quetzal, three wattled bellbirds or other even more exotic bird species. Nearby **Barú Volcano Park** is one of Panama's best areas for bird expeditions.

Hans & Terry van der Vooren lead groups on a variety of highland tours including bird trips, coffee farm visits and trips to see a Ngöbe Buglé Indian village. They lead groups in English, Spanish, Dutch and German.

There are plenty of good places to eat in the region, especially in the gringo-heavy Boquete area. Boquete is where most of the produce for Panama is grown. Beef production and fishing are also important in the area. This shows up on restaurant menus in the form of fresh vegetables, fruit, shrimp, langostas, corvina and filet mignon.

Barry, at the Coffee Estate Inn, is a wonderful reference for coffee facts and lore. He has been growing coffee and researching varietals at the inn for many years. He will suggest you take a trip to a coffee *beneficio*, or coffee-processing plant, which is certainly one of the top attractions of Boquete.

Beneficio **Café Ruiz** features their own, locally-produced products. The roadside shop is the starting and ending point for the company's tour of their nearby farm, *beneficio* and roasting operation. Wonderful, fresh roasted coffee is for sale for immediate consumption or for the road. Various roasts are available as well as examples of some of the more interesting local heirloom *típico* varieties. Ask for some geisha, currently the trendiest of coffee varieties.

With nearby **Volcán Barú**, mountain hiking simply doesn't get much better. A number of ancient Indian trails are still serviceable and are still in use by local Indians. Quetzal searches are one of the most popular ways to see the cloud forest and, hopefully, this very colorful bird that is the end-all and be-all for many birders.

The **Chiriquí Viejo**, **Rió Grande** and **Chagres** rivers offer everything from quiet floats to class IV and V rapids. Outfitters haul punters in vans to put in sites, usually a couple of hours away from lodging. Be sure to ask about river levels if there has been lots of rain. Aventuras Panamá offers several different trips for different levels of rafters.

After spending the morning exploring the highlands, make your way to the airport in David for the flight to Panama City. You'll probably arrive at Albrook Airport just before dark. Fortunately, it's only a short half-hour ride to birders' paradise, **Canopy Tower**.

If you feel like a splurge, book the **Harpy Eagle Suite** at Canopy Tower. This is where they put visiting celebrities. There are two beds and, by sleeping in one on the first night of my visit and the other bed the next night, I am assured to have slept in the same bed as Jimmy Buffett, Jimmy Carter, Martha Stewart and baseball legend Albert Pujols.

ALTERNATIVE PLAN

Rent a car in Boquete and take the day to drive back to Panama City at a leisurely pace. Stop at remote beaches and funky roadside eateries.

By international standards, the suite, as well as the rest of the rooms, rate about one star and cost about four stars. The accommodations are very bare bones, but the location and configuration of the tower make it well worth the high room prices. It's all about birds.

Days 5 and 6 – Canopy Tower

Start your morning early with hot coffee and a buffet breakfast. You'll need fuel to last through a full day of hiking to nearby holy spots like **Pipeline Road**, the **Ammo Dump** and **Semaphore Hill**.

The tower is an old radar tower situated on the top of one of the highest hills in **Soberanía National Park**, in the middle of profound rainforest. Each level of the tower gives guests the opportunity to observe the ecology of the forest canopy at a different level. **Monkeys**, **sloths** and zillions of **birds** flock around. The top level offers views out over the rainforest canopy to the canal.

Food is served at a buffet and is quite good—much better than the rooms. Guide services are simply the best in the world. This is serious birder territory, and hard-core birders come from all over the world to spend days out in the forest with the guides from Canopy Tower. The lodge employs some of the top bird guides on the planet to help their guests add hundreds of birds to their life lists.

Tours from Canopy Tower last a half or a full day. The hiking is not strenuous, and you don't generally cover a lot of territory, but if you're not really a nature lover, things can get a bit tedious. Twitchers will spend hours in one spot, obsessing over yet another LBB (Little Brown Bird), even going so far as to set up a portable table and chair to take notes.

Guides are outfitted with the very latest optical and electronic gadgets. They use iPods hooked up to small speakers on their belts to play back pre-recorded birdcalls, luring in difficult-to-see species for a close look. Laser pointers are great for guiding tired gringo eyes through the forest canopy to the nest in the tree with two ravenous harpy eagle chicks. This is birding at its very best.

Most of the birding excursions take place in or near **Soberanía National Park**, a 55,000-acre park that runs along the east side of the Panama Canal and consists of mountainous tropical rainforest. It is close to Panama City and has well developed trails, as well as two resorts bordering it. The famous birding site, **Pipeline Road**, is within the park. Over 400 bird species have been encountered in the 54,000-acre park. Birders will be looking for antshrikes, manakins, tanagers and rufous motmots.

Pipeline Road is a birding destination with a list exceeding 400 species. This overgrown maintenance road is the best place in the world to see tropical forest birds.

From time to time, the lodge offers slide shows, films and lectures in the evenings about guess what? Birds.

After a long day and evening spent viewing and talking about trogons and shrikes, go to bed early with visions of motmots dancing in your head.

Days 7 and 8 – San Blas

Once again, you'll need to wake up veeery early to catch an early flight. The flight to **El Porvenir** leaves at 6am, which means you need to arrive at Albrook about 5am.

The airport in El Porvenir is only a strip of crumbling asphalt. There is no actual arrival building or anything other than a few shacks, a police station and a dock. The island itself is not much more than a few acres in size.

A representative from **Coral Lodge** will meet you at the airport and escort you through arrival procedures (the police write your name and passport details down in a spiral notebook) and into a funky motor launch for a short trip to **Corbisky Island**. At this Kuna Indian village,

you will enjoy the hospitality of Elias Perez and his gracious wife, who will prepare a basic breakfast and allow you to admire and purchase some of her wonderful molas. After breakfast and shopping, you can go on a short tour of the village. The tour is short since the island only has a school, guesthouse (sort of), two churches and a dozen or so houses (sort of). You can peek into the village *congreso* where village elders spend evenings deciding issues of the day.

The villages, the islands themselves, and especially the women and young girls, are extremely photogenic. Be sure to ask permission before taking pictures of anyone—the Kuna are very sensitive about this and expect to be paid a minimum of $1 per person, per snap. They are serious about this. It may seem a little strange at first, but realize that the Kuna have few ways of earning money from the thousands of visitors who flock to their picturesque islands.

After you absorb the sights of the Kuna village, the launch will take you past dozens of tropical Edens to the remote and beautiful Dog Island. This is a spot of sand about 5 acres or so in size with a few coconut palms and a rim of white sand. The island is surrounded by the most beautiful blue water in the world. Picturesque Indians sail by in their *ulus*, dugout canoes, and colorful reef fish flit about in the shallows.

ALTERNATIVE PLAN

Lounge around the beach all day enjoying refreshing tropical beverages. A couple of half-hour snorkel excursions in the shallow water in front of the lodge can be followed by more beach time. Venture as far as the bar/dining area in the evening to gorge on seafood and Chilean wine.

This is a good spot for snorkeling, with a small wreck just a few feet off the beach. Lunch is served on an old coconut log. Beer and soft drinks can be consumed. There are a couple of hammocks strung up for naps. Good idea.

After a few hours lounging around on your Robinson Crusoe island, the launch will take you to **Coral Lodge**, where you can begin to enjoy a bit of luxury. You don't really need shoes here. Straight off the cover of a travel magazine, the Caribbean Sea and sky are almost overwhelming. You can swim from your room to breakfast or beer in a *bohío* perched on the reef. Romantic casitas are at the end of a long dock waaay out on the reef.

The lodge is the best base in the area for exploring the beautiful archipelago. The Kunas do not allow western-style development in their province. As a result, there are no western-style accommodations in the entire province. The few local guesthouses are extremely basic. Coral Lodge is located just outside the Kuna Yala Comarca, so you can stay in luxury and use the lodge's launches to explore the wonderfully picturesque islands.

Check in, consume umbrella drinks, veg out in a hammock, and nod off with visions of Kuna Indians dancing in your head.

In the morning, you can either do nature things within a mile or two of the lodge, or, once again, take the Lodge's launch on a tour through the beautiful San Blas Islands and check out other Kuna Indian villages.

Wonderful diving is found directly off the coast in front of Coral Lodge. The long barrier reef has been explored only slightly. Eric, the lodge manager, is a certified PADI dive instructor, and leads groups on dives at previously unexplored reefs. The mangroves and shallow reefs around the lodge are home to interesting species of birds, monkeys, colorful reef fish, sharks, rays, and unusual tropical creatures.

I always enjoy an evening spent trading stories over dinner and wine with other guests at a remote tropical lodge. Manager Eric Bauhaus is a gracious and well-traveled host who can hold his own when world travelers start telling tall tales.

Day 9 – Canal Train & Panama City Nightlife

On the last day at the lodge, guests usually leave at a reasonable hour in the morning and travel by launch along the coast to Miramar, where they are met and transported by road to Portobelo. A quick tour of the ruins (you don't really need much more than a half hour or so to see it all) is followed by lunch at the Coco Plum Restaurant on the sea.

After lunch, you can choose to ride back to Panama City by road, or take the quaint old **Panama Canal Railway Company** train that runs alongside the canal back to town. This is a great trip. The comfortable and picturesque old Canal Zone-era train leaves Colón at 5:30pm for the hour-long trip along the canal to Panama City. The cars are very comfortable and there are great, old-timey observation decks.

From the station in Panama City, take a taxi to your hotel. I suggest nearby **La Estancia B&B** for comfortable, inexpensive lodging in a quiet, residential neighborhood.

Dining in Panama City can mean choosing between fusions of a surprising number of cultures. Local seafood is tops. Add in influences from Spain, Asia and other Latin American countries and your selection of flavors to explore is fat.

In the old, now trendy part of town, Casco Viejo, **Manolo Caracol** is one of the most interesting dining choices in town. There is no menu—they just start bringing out the food and eventually place some 10 to 15 different courses in front of you. The performance is very simple, very elegant and very, very good. Grouper with garlic sauce: *estupendo*!

Go to bed early (I know, I know. I keep saying this) and rise before cock's crow to make the early flight from Albrook Airport to Bahía Piñas.

Daya 10, 11, 12 and 13 - Bahía Piñas

Waaaay down the Pacific coast, 18 miles from the Colombian border, in the wilds of Darien, **Tropic Star Lodge** is an oasis of civilization (luxury, actually) with nothing else around but jungle-covered mountains for miles. The mountains come right down to the sea and huge chunks of forest come crashing down into the spectacular, heavy surf from time to time.

The flight to Piñas Bay passes over the scenic Pearl Islands—well worth a look if the sky is clear. Bahía Piñas is a small Indian village with an airstrip, about 20 or 30 Indians and 50 policemen (the border with Colombia is nearby). A short ride in a jeep takes visitors to a gravel beach where you board a launch for the five-minute ride around the point to the lodge.

Even though it is amazingly remote, the lodge is certainly quite comfortable, bordering on luxury. The lodge and fishing are so good, it is almost 100% booked almost continually. Wealthy business executives, celebrities and fishing maniacs come from all over the world. More world records have been caught at Tropic Star Lodge than in any other location on the planet.

Fishing for marlin and sailfish on the nearby famous **Zane Grey Reef** is sensational. I describe Tropic Star Lodge in great detail in the *Best Sleeps & Eats* section and the fishing in *Best Activities*.

Day 14

Tropic Star usually flies its guests back to Panama City mid-morning. This leaves you enough time for enjoying a little more of Panama City before you have to go back to Ardmore. Indulge in some sort of enlightening activity in the afternoon, dine sumptuously in the evening and enjoy live music for one last night. Consider blowing the rest of your money at the casino. What the heck, it's your last night in town, anyw anyway.

If you simply must see something of the **Panama Canal** before you go (a very reasonable request), get a taxi or your driver to take you a short way out of town to the **Miraflores Locks Visitor Center**. For tourists, this is really the best part of the entire canal system. You get to see the locks in action up close. Huge ships glide past just inches from your fingertips. There are informative displays and a gift shop with trinkets for sale. The food in the restaurant is abysmal but the view of canal operations from the tables is great.

I like seafood prepared in imaginative ways, and one of my favorite places in Panama City for enjoying imaginative cooking is **Siete Mares**. It is intimate and romantic with soft lighting and comfortable chairs. **Sea bass**, *corvina*, is the star of the show along with a wide variety of interesting ceviches.

If you feel lively, **Seis**, on Calle Uruguay, is a late, late, late night dance club. **Kos Panama**, next to Hooters, also in Calle Uruguay, features hot DJs and scorching dancing. **Il Bocalino** near Hooters, is known for live flamenco. **Bodeguita** is a hot salsa club and hooker hang out. **Unplugged** is next to **Moods**—a good spot for 80s rock bands.

11. BEST SLEEPS & EATS

If you want to get close to nature but still have the comforts of luxury lodging and fine dining at the end of the day, Panama can accommodate you in almost all parts of the country. There is a wide variety of lodging, including wonderful rainforest lodges (*like Al Natural, photo below*) as well as big city business hotels. Surf camps, fishing lodges, birders' hideaways and beachfront romantic bungalows abound.

One of the most wonderful reasons to visit Panama is to eat. The combination of wide international influence, fresh local produce and seafood and plenty of well-off business types and retirees willing to pay means the country has plenty of truly great restaurants.

Lodging

Panama has a wide array of hotels: from remote five star luxury jungle and beach lodges to big city business hotels with helipads and conference centers. From beachfront hippie havens to rock star hideaways. From under $10 per night to over $1,000 per night (per person).

Lodging Prices

Prices quoted are for one double room for two people.

$$$$$, Luxury: $400 +
$$$$, First-class: $250-400
$$$, Midrange: $100-250
$$, Budget: $25-100
$, Backpacker: $25 or less

In almost any part of the country, comfortable, air-conditioned hotels are available at reasonable prices. With this plethora of choice, I suggest you take a little time and select places to stay that are full of character, out of the way or interesting for some reason.

Panama City can be a very tight hotel market. Even in low season with seemingly hundreds of new high-rise hotels coming on line every week, hotel rooms can be hard to come by. Businessmen from all over the world, as well as tourists, pack the town, so be sure to book your PC rooms well in advance.

In the rainy season, along the Caribbean coast, sand fleas can be irritating when the breezes die down. Citronella and Skin So Soft work for some. My vote goes to plain old bug spray with high percentages of DEET. This is probably not good for you if you use it in large quantities for long periods of time, but it works.

Some lodges are built in or near mangrove swamps, which can emit a rather foul smell at times. When the breeze blows, this is not a problem.

Food & Eating Out

Restaurant prices in Panama are similar to US prices but the food is usually better. Fortunately, the country's infrastructure doesn't lend itself well to distributing and using lots of frozen food. So restaurants tend to actually cook things rather than just heat up things delivered by the Sysco truck as they do in the US. And the seafood is wonderful.

The restaurant scene in Panama City runs from street-side *cevicherías* (raw, marinated seafood stalls) to candle-lit fine dining atop skyscrapers with views out to sea. Trendy restaurants come and go. Even the very best tables in town can be gone in the blink of an eye, replaced by someplace even trendier the next week.

Restaurant Prices

$$$$$, Over $25
$$$$, $12-25
$$$, $8-12
$$, $5-8
$, $5 or less

Typical Panamanian chow revolves around vegetables, meat, chicken and seafood, seafood, seafood. Local *típico* restaurants serve set daily meals, *comida corriente*, with your choice of fish, chicken or meat accompanied by rice, beans, *patacones* (smashed, deep fried, plantains—wonderful!) and hot sauce. Tropical fruits make the Panamanian dining experience even better. Mangoes, papayas, sweet pineapples and bananas only hint at the delights of some of the more exotic fruits like mocambo, namance or tamarind.

You may run into **Johnnycakes**, which are a cross between a hamburger bun and an English muffin. Nice when toasted for breakfast. And always order **ceviche** any time you see it on the menu (*see photo below*). Ceviche is made from chopped up raw seafood, usually shrimp, scallops, fish or squid, with onions, peppers, garlic, cilantro and lots of limejuice. The juice cooks the seafood after a couple of hours in the refrigerator. It's great served on crackers or toast. It's all over Panama. Delicious!

Restaurants are required by law to include a 10% tip and 5% tax on the bill. Most don't do this. Sometimes these extras are mentioned on the menu and sometimes they come as a surprise at the end of the meal.

PANAMA CITY

BEST SLEEPS

Panama City has a vast selection of hotels, from budget joints with three rooms to gleaming, big city business towers with hundreds of rooms and penthouse suites. You can spend almost any amount of money you want. In spite of this seeming plethora of hotels, do not assume you can simply pop into town and grab any hotel you want. Amazingly, all the hotels seem to be almost perpetually booked up. **Book well in advance**.

Intercontinental Crowne Plaza $$$$

This is one of the better deals in town for a large, big city-type hotel with all the services. It used to be a Holiday Inn but has been extensively updated. Still, it is not as fancy as some of the other high-end lodging options. It's right across the street from and overlooks the Catholic Church where Manuel Noriega took refuge when the Americans kicked him out. *Info: Avenida Manuel Espinosa Batista. www.ichotelsgroup.com; Tel. 507-206-5555.*

Intercontinental Miramar Panama $$$$$

The Miramar is an impressive, luxury high-rise hotel on the waterfront. It is a big city business hotel with all the goodies. The wonderful views out to sea and over the Panama City skyline are very impressive. You can watch the freighters passing in and out of the canal along the breakwater. The hotel seems to be full every time I have been there. Wedding receptions and business meetings fill the ballrooms. The lobby is often crowded with party guests in frilly dresses and little boys wearing uncomfortable suits and ties. It is a busy place with helicopters buzzing about landing at their two heliports. Service in the hotel and in the restaurants is always snappy. This is a very professional operation.

The rooms are large with good mattresses and high-quality linens. The pillows are fluffy, the bathrobes are thick and each room seems to have at least five phones scattered about. Rooms are stocked with a choice of foam or feather pillows. The bathroom comes with a large basket full of dozens of exotic toiletries and the large mini bars are choked with local and international goodies. Of course there is fine coffee in the rooms.

The pool is large, complicated and good for kids. They have a big, well-equipped exercise room. Even though they are right on the water, there is no beach. The marina takes up most of the waterfront.

The restaurant has a different theme each night, with Italian, Mexican, Asian, Panamanian and seafood specials. The food is quite good but tends to be a little high priced—not unusual in such a hotel. Part of what you pay is for convenience and style. The Sparkles Bar is plush and comfortable with views out over the bay. Drinks come with a small tray of peanuts and olives. Very civilized.

Business services are extensive. I found their in-room wireless internet service to be too weak to use. In my experience this is very typical—most hotels have not yet perfected the art of supplying wireless service to their rooms. The business center staff bent over backwards for me and treated me to free use of their computers for my stay since their in-room service would not work. Good deal.

The location is good if you are interested in carrying on in the clubs and bars of the Calle Uruguay entertainment district—it starts right across the street. You can crawl back to your hotel in the wee hours after a night of salsa and mojitos.

None of this comes cheap. This is probably the nicest hotel in a town bursting with well-off international businessmen. I cannot say they are overpriced. They are almost always full in this bustling city and the market rules. Bottled water in the rooms goes for a mere $5 but there is a gas station across the street where the same bottle goes for $0.75. Such is life in the big city. *Info*: *Avenida Balboa. www.miramarpanama.com; Tel. 507-206-8888.*

The Bristol $$$$

I find the Bristol to be rather stuffy, with a quaint British feel and great ambiance. But the staff can be rather aloof.

There is a small restaurant and they have several meeting rooms. The bar is very quiet and elegant, but overpriced at $7.35 for a glass of average Chilean red, but with a vast selection of interesting rums from around the Caribbean.

Rooms are large and comfortable with every standard amenity, but I found their much-touted butler service not up to snuff. Moments after arriving in my room, the butler arrived, promising coffee, ice, the Miami Herald newspaper in the morning, restaurant bookings and more. None of that happened. I simply never heard from him again, and his phone number was never answered. I had to flag down my own taxis, never saw a newspaper and never had any ice. The in-room, wireless internet costs $12.50 per day. Crazy.

Although the Bristol has a reputation as the best hotel in Panama City, it has a way to go before it lives up to the hype. Quite simply: it ain't worth the money. The Miramar Intercontinental, nearby, has nicer rooms and great views if you don't have to have the ambiance. *Info: Banking District, Avenida Aquilino De La Guardia. www.thebristol.com; Tel. 507-264-0000.*

BEST EATS

Siete Mares $$$

The name (Seven Seas) certainly implies seafood, and that's what you get. Siete Mares is very intimate and romantic with soft lighting and comfortable chairs. It's the kind of restaurant you can spend several hours in. Sea bass, *corvina*, is the star of the show along with a wide variety of interesting ceviches. Corvina thermidor is a wonderful choice. The intimate bar seems to attract a small crowd of flush business types. *Info: Calle Guatemala. Tel. 507-264-0144.*

Eurasia $$$$
Anywhere in the world, this would be one of the top restaurants in town. The restaurant is located in an old, upper class Panamanian home with lots of character. Very romantic. The service is impeccable. Waiters, doormen and bartenders wear starched white shirts. A security guard outside the front door escorts all guests to and from their taxis. Starters average $12 and mains average $15. Local seafood items include langostas in fancy little rolls with dates, nuts, mesclun and shaved Parmesan cheese. My main was a pork loin with fancy tamarind sauce and polenta and apple chunks. White-suited wait staff are very professional. Very hard to top this place. The dessert table runs $7.50 and includes more fancy cakes and pies than you can shake a stick at. They're good too. *Info*: *Bella Vista. Tel. 507-264-7859.*

Gaucho's $$
Dark tile floors and wrought iron set the mood. The place is usually loud and bustling, full of businessmen on expense account lunches. The steaks come from the US and are good. The ceviche is a good choice for starters. If you are in the mood for meat, this will do just fine. *Info*: *Calle Uruguay. Tel. 507-263-4469.*

Manolo Caracol $$$
One of the most interesting dining choices in town, Manolo Caracol does things sort of tapas style with a set meal of numerous courses for $16. There is no menu—they just start bringing out the food and eventually place some 10 to 15 different courses in front of you. Great seafood, interesting vegetables and choice morsels of pork and beef allow even the pickiest eaters to find plenty of fascinating and different items to gorge on. They have a great wine list with plenty of mouth-watering Spanish selections. The whole experience can take a couple of hours, including flan de la casa for desert. The performance is very simple, very elegant and very, very good. Grouper with garlic sauce: *estupendo*! The price is very reasonable for what you get. *Info*: *Casco Viejo, Avenida Central. www.manolocaracol.net; Tel. 507-228-0109.*

Mi Ranchito $$
It's hard to beat a night messing around on the Amador Causeway with your sweetie. There are lots of interesting places to eat and stroll. The

view of the legendary Panama City skyline is best enjoyed from this point of view. Mi Ranchito is a more or less *típico* restaurant with open sides so you can enjoy being on the Causeway. The food is okay, leaning towards shrimp and steak with *patacones* and rice. It's a little touristy with a live *típico* band but, the times I've been there, the other diners were a smattering of gringo tourists and a bunch of lovey-dovey Panamanian couples sitting very close together. Very romantic. Nice. *Info*: *Amador Causeway. Tel. 507-228-4909.*

THE PANAMA CANAL

BEST SLEEPS

The area around the old Canal Zone includes several stylish and comfortable places to stay. Lodging on the beach, in the jungle or in town is available within a few minutes cab ride from Panama City.

La Estancia $$

The most charming of Panama's B&Bs, La Estancia is located on the slopes of Cerro Ancon overlooking the canal and the Bridge of the Americas. Monkeys, sloths and innumerable birds lurk just outside your bedroom window. It's close to Albrook airport if you need a handy place for the night between flights.

But the best thing about La Estancia is the helpful people who run it. They are thoughtful and caring, planning tours and trips around the country for many of their guests. You could put your whole trip in their hands and be confident of having a good time. They've been in the country for years, so they know what visitors like and all the ins and outs of the tourism infrastructure. They have a good selection of molas and handicrafts for sale and can offer expert advice on what to buy, where to buy it and how much to pay. Esteban and Gustavo are very pleasant, quiet and willing to be helpful or just fade into the background—as you prefer.

The 10 tiled rooms are large and comfortably appointed. They have fans, AC, phones, TVs and good mattresses. They have a large suite with full kitchen facilities. There are three common areas with free wireless internet service, a piano and a guitar for the musically inclined. Breakfast is more than just bread and coffee. They have a small menu and will fry eggs, prepare pancakes, etc. Very nice.

The area is part of the old US Army Senior Officers housing. The building has been remodeled and is up-to-date. Things are quiet here—it's completely residential, so you'll have to take a taxi to town. But taxis are cheap. I prefer to stay somewhere quiet like this and ride into town. One of the best things about La Estancia is that it is very comfortable but relatively inexpensive, so you can save money that you might normally spend on a big city hotel, but still be a short cab ride away from the action. In my opinion, this is the best place to stay in Panama City—clean, comfortable, friendly, and well located—a real bargain. *Info*: *Balboa, Quarry Heights. www.bedandbreakfastpanama.com; Tel. 507-314-1604.*

Intercontinental Playa Bonita $$$$

Just a few minutes outside Panama City, this hotel is very quiet and isolated on its own long, picturesque beach. I don't know how many pools they have—I kept losing count. They have at least two for kids only, and they are nice ones with plenty of shallow areas and all sorts of nooks and crannies to explore.

Most rooms have great views out to sea. You can see ships waiting to go through the canal. They are well appointed with good mattresses, coffee makers, mini bars and other goodies.

The beach is of a more interesting variety than the Miami Beach white sand type. It's great for long walks peeking into tide pools watching crabs and small sea creatures. The water is a little on the murky side.

Meals are served in several restaurants. The main restaurant has large buffets with nightly themes: seafood, Mexican, Italian, Chinese. As in most luxury resorts, the food prices are a little on the high side. The wine selection is limited but includes a couple of the better Chilean standards.

There is an adequate business center with all the usual internet services. When I discovered that the in-room wireless service ($15 for 24 hours) did not work in my room as promised, the business center staff told me they would notify an engineer. Perhaps they did. I had to work in the lobby where I found the wireless connection to be adequate.

Be careful. The last time I checked, their web site had the wrong phone number. *Info*: www.playabonitapanama.com; Tel. 507-211-8600.

Canopy Tower $$$

For hard-core birders, a trip to Canopy Tower is like making a pilgrimage to Mecca is for Muslims. It is simply the holiest birder shrine in the world. The lodge is a converted radar tower on top of a hill in the middle of the rainforest (*see photo on page 48*). Rooms are on floors of the tower right at canopy level with the lounge/dining floor just above the canopy. The top deck has views for miles over the jungle of the Soberanía National Park (*see photo below*) and of the nearby Panama Canal. Visitors can view birds and wildlife at all levels of the surrounding rainforest.

The lodge is quite solidly booked most of the year, but the experience is not to be missed if you are even a little interested in birds. The guests are almost all rabid birders. It's great to hang out in the lounge and listen to them discuss their passion for birds. I love it. So do Jimmy Carter, Jimmy Buffett, baseball great Albert Pujol and Martha Stewart, among other famous types who visit.

Ask to stay in the harpy eagle suite and you'll be able to say you slept in the same bed as the above worthies.

The lodge employs some of the top bird guides on the planet to guide their guests to nearby holy spots like Pipeline Road, the Ammo Dump and Semaphore Hill. *Info*: *www.canopytower.com; Tel. 507-264-5720.*

Gamboa Rainforest Resort $$$$

Appealing to luxury vacation seekers and eco-tourists alike, the Gamboa is a large, deluxe lodge at the edge of the rainforest overlooking Gatún Lake. This is not a stinky rainforest ecolodge.

In the morning, as you can sip your coffee in your hammock on the balcony, the noise from thousands of birds drowns out normal conversation. The almost overpowering sound of the birds reminds me of the sound of a large crowd at a cocktail party.

Over 300 bird species have been identified on the grounds of the lodge itself. It's filthy with parrots and parakeets. Flocks of 50 zoom all around the pool. Howler monkeys hoot across the valley, serving as alarm clocks in the morning. Birders come from miles around to twitch in the resort's extensive grounds.

When I strolled the grounds early one morning, I saw agoutis, crocodiles and monkeys within a couple hundred feet of my room.

But birds aren't the only attraction of the resort. The activities offered are numerous: tennis, water polo, fishing for peacock bass, eco-walks in the rainforest, and more. The resort maintains a very interesting butterfly house, an orchid garden, and a snake house. They are well done and definitely worth a visit.

The resort was built in 2000 and includes 38 of the old managers' houses left over from the US canal days. They have been nicely remodeled and rent for much less than the rooms in the hotel—a bargain. For some reason, the floors in the main hotel building are numbered upside down: the top floor is #1 and the bottom floor is #5. Curious. Remember this when you get on the elevator.

The 200 tiled rooms are large, with balconies overlooking the lake. They are nicely appointed with all the comforts one expects in upscale resorts: bathrobes, hair dryers, ironing boards, in-room safes and baskets filled with goos and creams in the bathroom. They have several deluxe suites with multiple bedrooms, open bars and fresh flowers and fruit brought to the room daily.

The unique location and luxury appointments attract an upscale crowd, including celebrities like Jimmy Carter, Albert Pujol, Miss Universe and Chayanne (big time singer from Puerto Rico).

The food in the three restaurants is the weak link. The buffets are okay, but certainly not up to the standards of the rest of the resort. Some of the food on the buffet is good, but much of it is mediocre. Seafood, Italian and other international specialties are featured but I was served nothing of particular interest. The restaurant, in the main building, is billed as "gourmet," but at $35 for the set menu, most Americans would be disappointed. It's overpriced. Their best restaurant, the Lagarto, is a short ride from the main building on the banks of the Chagres River. The views are great but, once again, the food is forgettable. *Info: www.gamboaresort.com; Tel. 507-206-8888, 877-800-1690 (toll free, US).*

BEST EATS

Although you will see lots of **local roadside food stands** and the occasional restaurant, lodges and hotels in the area have the best meals. Don't expect anything real fancy. You'll have to go into town for that, but **Panama City is close**.

Meals for guests at the famous **Canopy Tower** are served buffet-style and are quite good. Gamboa Rainforest Lodge has three restaurants but I cannot recommend any of them.

BOCAS DEL TORO

BEST SLEEPS

Bocas del Toro offers a wide assortment of lodging choices but no real luxury options. Remote lodges are at one end of the scale and el cheapo backpacker hostels are at the other. Bocas Town is backpacker heaven with "backpacker beds" going for $8 (with breakfast). There are no upscale lodgings in town at all. Many hotels are right on the water with great views. Otherwise, the views will be depressing glimpses of third world backyards.

If you plan on taking tours and exploring the area, Bocas Town is a logical choice for a base. There are thousands of water taxis flitting about like bugs to a light at a barbeque and every tour imaginable is touted. Bocas Town has all the restaurants and all the nightlife. All of the remote lodges can arrange for tours but it can get rather expensive to go back and forth by water taxi. It may cost as much as $60 one-way to some of the lodges. Fares to ones even fairly close to Bocas Town run $10 or so. It can add up if you want to party late.

Most of the water taxis stop running at 11pm—just when the fun starts at most of the bars in town. Also, it's quite dangerous to be zooming around on the water at night, since many locals are out in their tiny *cayucas* with no lights. I heard several stories of families being run over.

Al Natural $$$

The white sand beach is very calm, good for swimming and snorkeling. The view from your bed (without lifting your head up off the pillow – *see photo on page 119*) is right out of a glossy travel mag—Caribbean perfection. Quiet, quiet, quiet. Very romantic—good for honeymooners. Good surfing spots and other, wilder, white sand beaches within a very short walk. Price includes three meals, wine with dinner and free use of kayaks and snorkeling equipment. The accommodations are open sided thatched roof jobs with hammocks, ceiling fans and romantic mosquito netting. You don't need air-conditioning or screens—the breeze blows right on through.

The resort organizes several unique tours to Zapatillas Islands, Red Frog Beach and other interesting nearby beaches and sights. Snorkeling trips go to several secret spots. Fishing and surfing excursions can also be arranged. The lodge/resort is quite isolated. It's about a 45-minute run to Bocas Town and they don't go after dark, so you need to get your hard partying done before or after you arrive.

The bar/dining room/hang out spot is a large bohío with a lookout tower and good assortment of essential boozes. There are lots of European guests. The place is run completely on solar power, and drinking and bathing water is filtered rainwater. There is plenty to do here if that's what you want. You could just hang out in hammocks and swill rum too—more my style. I liked the place a lot when I was there. I especially enjoyed conversations with the enthusiastic and wonderfully outgoing owner, Belgian Michel Natalis. I must mention that I found the place to be getting a little run down and in need of maintenance—but still wonderful. *Info: Bocas del Toro. www.alnaturalresort.com; Tel. 507-757-9004.*

Bocas Inn $$
Aimed mostly at budget travelers, this is the nicest place in town. The rooms are small and basic but quite clean and adequate. The air-conditioning works fine and the water is hot. There is a wonderful deck and lounge area where you can sit in either shade or sun and watch the world go by. It's right on the water and very conveniently located. I don't really like to stay any closer to town, but it's still only a five-minute stroll to the bars and nightspots.

Ancon Expeditions (the best tour operator in Panama) runs this place mostly for housing their groups signed up for expeditions around the archipelago, but anyone can book a room. They offer the best-run tours in the area with well-trained guides and fairly new boats. The Inn is on the north side of town, an adequate distance away from the wildness of the bars right in the middle of things.

Meals can be arranged in advance and are quite tasty. Given the wide range of interesting restaurants within a short walk, it makes sense to eat breakfast at the Inn and sample the fish joints for lunch and dinner. *Info: Bocas del Toro. www.anconexpeditions.com; Tel. 507-269-9415.*

Punta Caracol Acqua-lodge $$$$

A little more professionally run than the other resorts in Bocas del Toro, the Caracol is nicely upscale. Wait staff wear white jackets, perform discreetly and with polished competence. Someone has obviously trained the staff to be on their best behavior. No shouting or loud reggaeton blaring. You don't see the staff napping in the dining room or yakking loudly when they should be hustling drinks. When you order a beer, they don't just bring you the bottle. They ask if you would like it with a glass, with ice, etc. They seems a little disturbed if you just want to suck it down straight from the can.

The over-the-water casitas are attractively decorated with native wall art and ceramics. They are very comfortable with ceiling fans and upstairs bedrooms. Everything runs on solar power. The upstairs bedrooms get hot at night so take off the top of the mosquito netting and turn on the ceiling fan.

Prices include breakfast and dinner. A menu with three or four choices for each dinner course is presented early in the day for you to make your choice. Individual tables. Big menu for lunch, including a variety of interesting salads, pasta, fish dishes and hamburgers. Vegan choices appear at every meal.

Overall, the restaurant does a nice job but they fall short of fine dining. My pargo filet was great but full of bones. The "tropical fruit crepe" turned out to be a crepe filled with regular-old fruit cocktail complete with grapes and cherries with some sort of watered down strawberry jelly on top.

You can snorkel right from your unit. Cute, colorful local dugout canoes are available for your paddling pleasure. Trips to town can be arranged to suit your needs running well into the night, so you can party in town and return for whatever.

Although not quite in the luxury category, this is the most comfortable lodging option. It's not far from town and is fairly quiet and isolated. Not funky as are almost all the other lodging options. You can keep to yourself if you like or hobnob with the other guests. Safes, ceiling fans, no AC, no regular electricity, no internet, but you can make a phone call if needed. All the usual tours can be arranged. If you want to see the area and do all the great tours nearby, and a funky Caribbean beach resort with group meals is not your style, this is your best option. *Info*: *Bocas del Toro. www.puntacaracol.com; Tel. 507-6612-1088.*

Garden of Eden Resort $$$

With only three rooms, on a tiny island all by itself, it would be hard not to relax at this peaceful and comfortable resort. It is extremely quiet and private yet only 15 minutes by water taxi from the fleshy delights of Bocas Town.

The rooms are large and comfortably appointed with hot water, showers and hammocks on the balcony. You can gaze out over the blue Caribbean waters without lifting your head up from your pillow. Ceiling fans keep the air moving. No AC. You don't really need it.

The resort is only a year old and has been lovingly crafted by owners Robert and Helena Myers. Retired from a life of contracting and fishing around Big Pine Key in Florida and the corporate world, the Myers have

created an atmosphere of tranquility and laid-back island life. They bring a refreshing air of the Keys to the whole experience. If you nag him, Bob might take you fishing. March, April and May are prime time for tuna. Helena can can economically arrange all of the usual area tours. Restorative massages are offered by the talented Señora Talita.

Not only is the Garden of Eden rated number one in Bocas del Toro by posters on TripAdvisor.com, it is a stone cold bargain. Rooms for two go for $120 per night. The rate includes breakfast and transportation to and from Bocas Town every day (this is a $20 value). Typical meals include very large portions of steak, lobster, shrimp and local vegetables. Their most expensive lunches go for around $6 and their famous steak and lobster dinner is a mere $20. Beer is $1 and umbrella drinks $3. Good Chilean wines go for $16 a bottle. So you're not stuck on a small island paying fancy resort prices for your consumables. Don't miss the smoked kingfish dip.

One of the best things about the place is the owners. One glance tells you this is a place to relax and chat with old pals while sipping interesting rum concoctions late into the night. One of the reasons they chose this lifestyle is their love of having friends over to hang out and relax. You are their friends.

The grounds are meticulously manicured and loaded with exotic heliconias, orchids, ginger plants and other fantastical tropical plants. The small pool and patio are private, suitable for even the most daring sun worshippers. The sparkling pool is the cleanest I have seen in Panama. Very inviting! Stroll to the end of the dock and you can see hundreds of snapper that Helena pampers with kitchen scraps. Julie, a 10-lb. jewfish, lurks about. There is a sandy area with lounge chairs, but no beach. But still, the swimming is good and the snorkeling right around the island is rewarding.

Kayaks are free and the surrounding area is great for exploring. You can paddle to nearby white sand Red Frog Beach for lounging around or surfing.

Book early. This is, by popular vote, the nicest place to stay in the Bocas del Toro area. It's only a year old but the secret is already out. My educated guess is that they will be solidly booked by 2008. *Info*: *Isla Solarte. www.gardenofedenbocaspanama.com; Tel. 507-6487-4332.*

BEST EATS

You can certainly eat well in Bocas. Bocas Town has a wide selection of funky restaurants to choose from, but nothing even approaching fancy. Fish, fish and more fish is the deal. Some of the restaurants are located right on, or even over, the water. A leisurely lunch in the shade watching the boat traffic on the waterfront is a lovely way to spend a couple of hours. Realize that, in Bocas, you can never really get away from the booming reggae no matter what you do.

You'll certainly end up with Johnnycakes at some point (usually breakfast). These are a cross between a hamburger bun and an English muffin. They're pretty good when toasted or warm from the oven.

If you are staying at one of the remote lodges you're pretty much stuck with what they have. There are few restaurants outside town. Expect only a few, sometimes wonderful, fish joints. Most lodges serve family style and few offer much selection. Fish and spiny lobster are the deal.

Lemon Grass $$$

Interesting seafood specials run to Pac rim standards like Thai pargo, curried goat and jerked chicken. The beer is cold and the view, if you insist on a good table, is great. *Info*: *Bocas Town, Calle 1.*

Ultimate Refugio $$$
This is a gringo refuge catering to an interesting mix of short-term tourists and assorted gringos going to seed. Seafood, pasta, guacamole and other Mexican standards make up the menu. *Info: Bocas Town.*

El Limbo On the Sea $$
Wonderful location on a deck just two feet over the sea overlooking the busy waterfront. It would be hard to find a nicer location to eat lunch in Bocas Town. Other than that, it's forgettable. The menu runs to about 25 pages and includes salmon, trout, crepes, pizza, pages and pages of salads and a couple of fish items. Fried fish with all the trimmings and a couple of local beers cost me $12. Not bad but I'm hoping for better. *Info: Bocas Town, Calle 1, in the hotel of the same name.*

Om Cafe $$
The Om is probably the most interesting place to eat in town, and my favorite. If you have tired of seafood, Om has Indian cuisine fit for a Maharaja. The vindaloo is hot but the tikka massala is perfect for most palates. They serve most of their dishes with a choice of chicken, fish or shrimp. Entrees come with nan and daal. They have spectacular lassis (Indian milk shakes) and wonderful juice combinations. They offer a dozen or so types of juice and let you pick a blend. *Info: Near the park but look for signs. The location changed recently.*

SAN BLAS ARCHIPELAGO

BEST SLEEPS
There are very few lodging options in the San Blas, and none of them are more than very basic tourist accommodations. The **Kuna Indian tribe** tightly runs the province, and they do not allow outsiders to operate businesses within their borders. Local Kunas own and run the few very basic hotels and restaurants. The word "comfortable" would be stretching things a bit.

However, the wonderful Coral Lodge is located right at the western border of the province. It's a good base, so you can stay in comfort and beauty and explore the Kuna Yala in the lodge's launches.

> **Wild Ride!**
>
> One recent 20-mile boat trip I took from my lodge was so rough, it was impossible to remain sitting down on the padded seat. Tropical rain poured on us for the entire two-hour trip. I cracked a rib banging against a stanchion, and arrived shivering and soaked completely from head to toe with water sloshing around in my shoes. At least my luggage was dry. Great fun!

Hospedaje Corbisky $
Helpful and friendly Elias Perez and his wife have six basic rooms for rent at $30 per night on **Corbisky Island**—just a short boat trip from El Porvenir. It's right in the middle of a fairly typical Kuna Indian village. All meals are included and consist of very basic fare: rice, fish, yucca and eggs. If you want to get a good feel for how the local population lives, this is your chance. Bring mosquito repellent and be prepared for some inconveniences.

The village is very tightly packed. Bathroom facilities are of the most basic sort imaginable. The toilet is a hole in the floor over the water—with no intermediaries. Washing is done at a large plastic barrel filled with rain collected from the roof. This is typical Kuna life. The village is not particularly clean and I found some of the people, women especially, to be rather pushy. *Info*: *Corbisky Island. Tel. 507-6708-5254.*

Coral Lodge $$$$
You don't really need shoes here. Straight off the cover of a travel magazine, the Caribbean Sea and sky are almost overwhelming. You can swim from your

room to breakfast in a bohío perched on the reef. Romantic casitas are at the end of a long dock waaay out on the reef.

They have a nice pool, kayaks, wireless internet, and great food and wine. I found the manager and staff to be pleasant and professional. Colorful fish flit about all around you. It's just you and the sea. *Info*: El Porvenir. www.corallodge.com; Tel. 507-202-3795.

BEST EATS

Unless you are staying at **Coral Lodge**, where the food falls into the fine dining category, food in the Kuna Yala will be a big disappointment. There simply are no facilities in the area for preparing and serving food for visitors. Fish, rice, eggs and bananas are pretty much what's on the menu. You will be offered spiny lobster the Indians pick from their remaining reefs. None of the food is well prepared.

GULF OF CHIRIQUÍ

BEST SLEEPS

There are only a few lodging options but a couple of them are real standouts.

Islas Secas Resort $$$$

This is, without a doubt, the nicest place to stay in Panama. None of the other resorts or lodges come close. I have stayed at luxury lodges all over the world and this one takes the cake.

I am always skeptical when remote lodges bill themselves as "luxury". Luxury is not easy to do when everything needed has to be brought in by boat or small plane. These guys have it though: fluffy bathrobes, fluffy pillows, big fluffy towels, elegant furnishings, trendy food, fine wines, personal service, etc.

But that's not what makes Islas Secas so special. The islands and the sea around them are simply beautiful. Remote hardly describes the setting. There is no one here but the few resort staff and a few guests. There are 16 islands in the archipelago—all owned by the resort. The islands are miles and miles from anywhere.

Rumor has it, Mick and the boys stay here from time to time. The manager admitted to me that celebrities come and stay, but he refused to name names. Good for him.

Guests are housed in six *casitas* (small houses). These are Pacific yurts, which are largish, round structures with screened windows all around. All of the casitas are situated waaaay by themselves on top of small promontories with fabulous views out over the Pacific. The honeymoon yurt is all by itself on its own small island. Couples are sometimes not seen for days as they slide into the romantic surroundings and indolent lifestyle that quickly absorbs them.

There are no sounds except for the wind through the trees and the gentle lapping of waves on the beach. A few birds twitter about. Water is from a deep island well and is plentiful and sweet. Gravel paths connect the casitas with the restaurant/bar area and meander throughout the island. Each casita has its own solar power system, fans and lights. The largest has a fully stocked kitchen.

Of course luxury means different things to different people. In a remote lodge, if you want the luxury of air-conditioning, you will have to put up with the sound of a generator. Even if it is at the other end of the lodge, you will be able to hear it a little and it will drown out the sounds of nature. If you want the luxury of silence, skip the generator and rely on solar power. This means no AC. However, in many places a sea breeze and ceiling fans mean you don't really need the AC. The sounds of nature come through loud and clear.

Islas Secas has no phones, no TV (not even in the bar), no hair dryers, and no distractions. They do have a good wireless internet connection and the manager has a cell phone for emergencies.

It's very quiet, very casual. I spent my whole stay in the same pair of swimming trunks, only adding a T-shirt and flip-flops for meals.

Everything is included in the room rate: accommodations, all meals and snacks, kayaking, snorkeling, scuba diving, boat excursions, surfing, whale watching excursions, local fishing and cocktails. Tips are also included. The only things not part of the deal are the extensive spa treatments and offshore sport fishing.

If you want to go on a picnic and hang around at a remote, white-sand beach, they'll pack your lunch and drop you off where absolutely no one else is around. You can take off your clothes and run around naked—no problem. Islas Secas gives you the option of being all alone, but pampered if you like.

Diving in the area is simply the best in Panama. Kieron Boudains, the lodge manager is a certified diving instructor and has been diving in the area for many years. He knows where all the hot spots are. Most of the dive sites he takes guests to are never visited by anyone else.

Spa treatments include sea salt and brown sugar scrubs, a wide variety of massages and aromatherapy. I suggest the massage medley, which includes aromatherapy, acupressure, Swedish massage and any of the other treatments that appeal to you. This goes for $100. Not a bad deal.

Food is truly gourmet quality. The chef, Alexander Rojas, trained at Eurasia in Panama City and has spent time recently in Spain, picking up new recipes and some of the best of the new trends in international cuisine. He is considered to be one of the top two or three chefs in the country.

Drinks of all types are always included. This is not the usual all-inclusive deal with cheap boozes. The included booze is international quality, with wines much better than the usual run-of-the-mill California chardonnay and Chilean red stuff. Imaginative umbrella drinks are part of the deal. If you like, the staff will bring bottles of your favorite tipple, mixers and snacks to your room whenever you like. It's all included.

During the dry season, guests are flown to the islands from Albrook airport. Green season guests are brought by small boat from the port near David. The hour and a half boat ride down the Pedregal River and across the Gulf of Chiriquí is a great adventure in itself. *Info*: *www.islassecas.com; Tel. 800-377-8877 US.*

Panama Big Game Sportfishing Club $$$$

A remote, comfortable lodge perched at the edge of some of the best fishing grounds in Central America. A visit to Panama Big Game is the dream of every red-blooded angler wanting to do battle with billfish and exotic tropical fish species.

I was lucky enough to spend four days on the water at Panama Big Game this September taking pictures for New Jersey boys Ron Torkas and Joe Ozalas. Wahoo to 50 lbs. were everywhere. I lost count early on. Small yellow fin tuna were hitting on top water—exciting action! Lots of small dorado, yellow snapper, blue jack, bonito, and rainbow runners kept the boys busy with too many jack and houndfish to keep track of. Oh yeah, we ran into a couple of marlin too.

We fished four full days with Captain Tati and mate Eddie in a 31' Bertram. Most of the time we fished near pinnacles in the area of Montuoso, but we also visited Islas Secas for roosterfish and Los Ladrones for snapper. Poor Ron and Joe hardly had time to fish for marlin with all the wahoo action. "No more wahoo!" was the final decision. This cleared the decks for serious marlin battles. Early on day three, we arrived at Montuoso, quickly landed five bonito for bait and dropped them over with a couple of live blue runners for variety. Joe hooked up with a marlin almost immediately, fought for about 45 minutes and released a black weighing in the 350 lbs. neighborhood.

We had barely recovered when Ron hooked another black. After about a half hour fighting the marlin in the pouring rain, Ron released his black, also running about 350 lbs. We spent the rest of the day bottom bumping for huge snapper and casting surface plugs for tuna. Not bad for the off-season.

We usually arrived back at the lodge by 5:30 or 6:00, showered and spent the rest of the evening gorging on Lee's sushi, ceviche, home cooking, drinking rum and telling lies. Great fun! The rooms are large, air conditioned, with king-size beds and the showers have plenty of hot water. The minibars are kept chock full of beer and Cokes (no extra charge).

I don't know why anyone would call August/September the "off" season. It rained on us once during the day, the weather was reasonably cool, and there was no one else fishing anywhere in the area. The seas boiled with life. We probably could have nailed more marlin but the boys wanted to taste everything the area had to offer. *Info*: *Boca Chica. www.panamabiggamefishingclub.com; Tel. 507-6627-5431, 786-600-1672 US.*

BEST EATS

There are plenty of *típico* restaurants in the small towns along the shore and a few fish joints on the beaches but, in general, visitors to the area end up eating in their lodges. Prepare yourself for a double helping of seafood—that's what the area specializes in.

THE CENTRAL HIGHLANDS

BEST SLEEPS

Canopy Lodge $$$

This major birding lodge is in the middle of one of the most picturesque valleys in the highlands. It sits above a small town in the cloud forest. Birders flock to see more than 500 species commonly found in the surrounding areas. The 150-acre grounds of the lodge itself teem with birds and exotic flowers. A babbling stream runs through the place almost, but not quite, drowning out the sounds of hundreds of birds that fill the grounds.

The rooms in the two-year-old lodge are quite comfortable. There is no AC, but the high altitude makes this unnecessary. Food is good, served buffet-style on long tables shared by all of the guests.

Serious birders spend hours after dinner discussing and cataloguing their finds from hikes on nearby trails. The lodge has two of the very best bird guides in the country on hand. Guests usually combine a visit here with a visit to the company's sister lodge, Canopy Tower just outside Panama City, to round out their Panamanian bird watching experience. The lodge is almost a secret. There is no sign on the road in front and it is not heavily marketed. In spite of this almost-anonymity, the lodge is usually full of serious birders from around the world. Many guests I met had made multiple trips to birding Meccas like Ecuador, Brazil and Peru. The knowledgeable guides and tour leaders show films and give educational lectures on rainy afternoons. Hard core twitchers ignore the rain and go birding anyway.

No birder, I spent a morning with guide Faustino Sanchez (Tino) just strolling around the grounds and on nearby trails, and spotted more than one hundred species. Remarkable! *Info*: *El Valle. www.canopylodge.com; Tel. 507-264-5720, US 800-930-3397.*

The Coffee Estate Inn $$$
Spanking clean and elegant, the Coffee Estate Inn is a small mountainside inn set in 6 acres of carefully tended tropical plantings and hundreds of coffee trees.

The location is high above Boquete with fabulous views of the mountains and valley. There are three quietly isolated bungalows and the rooms are some of the nicest I've seen in Panama. They are elegant and absolutely modern. They have TV, wireless internet and kitchens with full gourmet coffee making ability for serious java hounds.

The Canadian owners have a passion for fine coffee, and grow several varieties of *típica*, heirloom and modern hybrid beans. They roast their beans on site and make their fabulous coffee available to guests. I enjoyed a wonderful educational stroll through their grounds with owner Barry. He spent several hours telling me about growing and preparing coffee beans and about the coffee business in general. Fascinating!

Dinner is prepared on special request so be sure you make the request. The food is wonderful. Even though she only cooks on a small scale, mostly for her own guests, Jane is one of the best chefs in the country. The Inn's reputation for fine dinners is well deserved. Gourmands drive from Panama City just for her dinners.
What a great website! It's a good place to look for Panama travel information.

Many guests fly into the country and come straight to Barry and Jane, who are very familiar with the country and help their guests plan their time and make arrangements for their in-country travel. *Info*: *Boquete. www.coffeestateinn.com; Tel. 507-720-2211.*

Royal Decameron $$$$
Perhaps the most famous lodging in Panama, the all-inclusive beachfront Decameron is (and this is a puzzle to me) one of the most popular

destinations in the country. Everything is included: meals, drinks, water sports toys, even cigarettes. Simply hold up your hand with fingers set in a smoker's "V" and, magically, a cigarette will appear in it. No extra charge. It's like a cruise ship on land.

While an all-inclusive is a good choice for many tourists, the format tends to encourage the cattle-like operations of large hotels handling hundreds of tourists. The quality of the buffets is a small step above high school cafeteria food. Drinks are mixed with local boozes and can be weak unless you befriend the bartender. Crowds at prime dining times can be a put-off.

The beach is quite a nice one, long and sandy. Local seafood shacks and drink stands can be found at either end. There are several pools and a variety of resort sports are available. Rooms are reasonably comfortable with air-conditioning and all the usual goodies expected in a three star place. They have golf, a spa and a casino.

I find the hotel to be rather impersonal and cold. Some staff have the glazed look in their eyes that comes after months and months of ever changing tourist faces demanding instant service or advice for fun. Still, this is one of the most popular destinations in Panama. *Info*: *www.decameron.com; Tel. 507-215-5000.*

BEST EATS

There are plenty of good places to eat in the region, especially in the gringo-heavy Boquete area. Boquete is where most of the produce for Panama is grown. Beef production and fishing are also important in the area. This shows up on restaurant menus in the form of fresh vegetables, fruit, shrimp, langostas, corvina and filet mignon.

Coffee Estate Inn $$$$

The best meals in Boquete, by far, are the dinners prepared at the Coffee Estate Inn. They usually only cook for their guests but, if you call well ahead, they may include you in one of their elegant and famous evenings of fine dining and fine coffee. *Info*: *Boquete. www.coffeestateinn.com; Tel. 507-720-2211.*

Machu Pichu $$$

This well-known Peruvian favorite is quiet and appealing, with a large menu heavy on seafood. Chef Aristóteles' specialties are always a good choice. *Info*: *Avenida Belisario Porras. Tel. 507-264-9308.*

El Zaranya $$$

Boquete now has a Lebanese restaurant with all the expected pita, hummus, baba ghanoushs, sambusek, estifas and skewered meats with rice. Their menu is huge. *Info*: *Downtown Boquete.*

Deli Barú $$$

This is a great deli with all the expected meats, cheeses, pickles, breads and interesting bottled drinks. They do up great sandwiches. *Info*: *Downtown Boquete.*

Delicias del Peru $$$

Ceviche Peruviana and fried ceviche are the specialties here. Heavy on seafood, they have good entrees and soups. *Info*: *Just past the folklore museum in Boquete.*

DARIEN

BEST SLEEPS

Other than the luxury fishing lodge, Tropic Star, there really are no places to stay in Darien other than the rustic lodges operated by Ancon Expeditions. Their lodges are comfortable and located in some of the most pristine tropical forest areas in Latin America—well worth a visit.

Tropic Star $$$$$

I've stayed at dozens of fishing lodges around the world, and find that Tropic Star easily deserves its international reputation as the top fishing lodge in the world. Home to over 200 world records, the lodge is waaaay out in the middle of nowhere—National Geographic country for sure.

They have their own airport. It is extremely difficult to support an 18-room luxury lodge so far from the rest of civilization, but these guys have been doing it for over 50 years now.

The air-conditioned rooms, pool, grounds and meals are all top quality by any measure. The service is about as good as you will find anywhere.

A stay at Tropic Star is not cheap. The facilities are top-quality and deep-sea fishing uses a lot of fuel. So do running the massive generators and hauling supplies in from Panama City. The quality of the fishing makes the price seem small. Understand that this is a *fishing* lodge. There's not much else to do other than fish. Celebrities and the hardest of the hard-core anglers from all over the world come here and pay the price. Book well in advance since they are rarely less than 100% full.

Fishing is aimed primarily at billfish. Black, blue and striped marlin are reliable and multiple sailfish hookups are common. You can't beat a by catch of dorado, tuna, wahoo, roosterfish and seemingly zillions of other tropical game and table fish. See *Best Activities* for more information about fishing at Tropic Star.

When I returned hot and tired from my first long day fishing at the lodge, I was pleased to pass through the bar on my way to a hot shower and clean clothes and grab a quick beer. A couple of fellow anglers were enjoying the lodge's special appetizers: hot fish fingers from today's catch and homemade potato chips. Delicious! I grabbed a couple of bites and headed to my room and shower. I took the last half of my beer in the shower with me. When I got out I distinctly thought I smelled those fish fingers I'd tasted at the bar. There on the coffee table in my room was another cold beer and an entire plate full of piping hot fish fingers and potato chips. Now that's good service. *Info: Bahía Piñas. www.tropicstar.com; Tel. 507-250-4186.*

Cana Field Station $$$

Operated by Ancon Expeditions of Panama and reachable only by charter flight, this lodge consists of not much more than 8 double cabins, a dining hall with observation deck and two bathrooms. Sounds dreadful but it's not. There is hot water and the food is good. The area is regarded as one of the top two or three birding sites in the world. Birders and serious outdoor enthusiasts make up almost all of the guests.

Ancon arranges 5- and 8-day trips accompanied by one of their naturalist/guides. If you are a nature lover and outdoorsy type, you will love the place. There's not much there except for a system of trails into the surrounding mountainous jungle. The hard core among the guests can spend a night or two high in the cloud forest at the Pirri Tent Camp. This is the trip of a lifetime. *Info*: *Darien National Park. www.anconexpeditions.com; Tel. 507-269-9415.*

Punta Patiño Lodge $$$

Ancon Expeditions of Panama's Punta Patiño Lodge is located on a bluff overlooking the Pacific with hundreds of square miles of primary and secondary tropical forest behind. Guests can explore a varied set of marine and coastal environments with nearby wetlands, rivers and Embera Indian communities. Ancon's guides are some of the best trained anywhere. This is harpy eagle territory. Birders flock here from around the world, sure to add significantly to their life lists.

Better than rustic, the 10 cabins are air-conditioned and quite comfortable. All have private bathrooms. The dining hall serves up groaning buffets of wonderful food. *Info*: *Punta Patiño Nature Preserve. www.anconexpeditions.com; Tel. 507-269-9415.*

BEST EATS

The Darien lodges described here provide all meals and beverages. I loved the food at all of them and gained weight even though I was hiking or fishing for hours every day.

The food at Tropic Star is superb. Dinner is served from a menu provided for guests to choose from at breakfast. Fish from the day's catch feature prominently. Ancon's lodges serve food on a buffet and it is quite high quality.

12. BEST ACTIVITIES

Panama offers good shopping for *molas,* ceramics and baskets. Outdoor sports and recreation possibilities include sunning on tropical beaches, angling for marlin, whale watching and searching for the elusive resplendent quetzal on the slopes of Vúlcan Barú. Nightlife in Panama City sizzles, and Bocas Town offers young people puzzling delights like pogoing up and down all night to bass-heavy, skull-numbing rock.

This chapter is for anyone who comes to Panama to "do" something. Even if that something is limited to pool- and bar-side activities only, this chapter tells you where to go and how to do it best.

PANAMA CITY

The best way to enjoy a short stay in Panama City is to hire an English-speaking driver. You can hire almost any cab in town for $10 an hour, but most drivers speak only fair English, if any. I suggest you call José, who will arrange for local drivers with excellent English. He gets $12 an hour but it's worth it. I've used several of his drivers to haul me around town and even out into the country some. José also offers airport pick-ups for two people at $25. Not bad.

I've used several of his drivers and had a great time with them. Their English was very good and they took me to all sorts of places I would never thought of on my own (including a drive by ex-strongman Noriega's house). It's cheaper and much less hassle than renting a car. *Info: Panama City. Tel. 507-6614-7811.*

SHOPPING

While not exactly an international shopping destination, Panama City has one of the best shopping experiences in Latin America, with plenty of modern, trendy stores.

There are two large modern malls with hundreds of shops. Albrook Mall (*photo at right*) is more or less across the street from the domestic airport and next to the new, modern bus terminal. The MultiCentro Mall is more centrally located on Avenida Balboa. Both malls have several levels of shops and the usual barfsome food court emporiums. There are banks, ATMs and lots of shops selling sunglasses and sports clothes.

Panama hats are often sought out by visiting gringos. While you certainly can buy lots of Panama hats in Panama, the best ones are actually made in Ecuador. The national hat of Panama is the slightly less stylish *sombrero pintado*, or "painted hat". These are great for keeping the sun out of your eyes. You will occasionally see a Panamanian wearing a Panama hat, but the vast majority of Panama hat wearers are not Panamanians. No problem.

Felipe Motta

An impressive selection of over 1,000 wines makes Motta's as good a wine store as you will find anywhere. There are three branches in town. The main one is in Marbella. *Info*: *Tel. 507-302-5555.*

Panaphoto

Just around the corner from the Hotel Bristol, Panaphoto is a large consumer electronics store with a variety of computer and photographic equipment and supplies. They also sell small and large appliances and cell phones. This would be a good place to pick up a cheap phone for local use. Interestingly, they do not sell film. *Info: Calle 50, Calle 49. Tel. 507-263-0102.*

Flory Saltzman Molas

If you want to buy molas, this is the place to do it. The prices are, for the most part, better than you will find in San Blas, and the selection is incredible. Flory's daughter runs the place now, and she has literally thousands of molas to choose from. She is extraordinarily helpful and pleasant, and makes you very comfortable with the buying process.

There is no hard sell here, and she has a good selection of the highest quality molas. She has used or poor quality molas from $2.50 and the really nice ones, sewn together into large wall hangings can go for as much as a couple of hundred dollars. Many of her molas are already prepared with a backing and straps for wall hangings or for stuffing for throw pillows. This is the real deal. *Info*: *Just in front of Hotel El Panama. Via Veneto, Via España. www.florysmola.com; Tel. 507-223-6963.*

NIGHTLIFE & ENTERTAINMENT

Panama City is famous for late night partying, dancing, live music and elegant casinos. Note: What locals call "nightclubs" are usually what we in the US refer to as strip clubs.

Watering Holes

The bars at both the Decapolis Hotel and the Bristol are elegant, big city bars with good selections of rum from around the region and are worth checking out. **Buzz Panama** is an upscale club in Paitilla near the Super 99. **Bodeguita** in Calle Uruguay is a hot salsa club and hooker hang out. **Unplugged** in Calle Uruguay next to **Moods** is a good spot for 80s rock bands.

Casinos

Casino gambling is legal in Panama. There are 36 legal casinos countrywide, and 23 of them are in Panama City. Fancy Las Vegas style palaces (almost) compete with down-at-the-heels joints and everything in between. Games are a little different than stateside, so bone up on the rules before laying down your bets. At most city casinos, nothing much starts happening before 11pm. A few casinos, such as the **Veneto**, are magnets for interesting young women looking for interesting (and big spending) gringos.

Many tourists come to Panama specifically to meet willing Latinas for a short, shall we say, "friendship." Casinos seem to be one of the better places for a hookup, but standard houses of ill repute do exist.

El Panama is one of the glitziest casinos. *Info: Via Veneto, Via España.* Another is the **Veneto**, with all the usual slots and 42 table games. Interesting ladies flock here late in the evening. This is a hot spot for late night encounters. *Info: El Cangrejo.*

Nightclubs

As noted above, these are usually strip clubs. Beautiful women dance around a vertical pole whilst **wearing little or nothing**. There is generally a cover charge and drinks are priced high. Ladies expect tips to come by and "dance" at your table (or in your lap). Panama City's nicer nightclubs include the **Cotton Club** on Via España next to McDonald's. It is a newish, glitzy strip club run by Americans. $25 gets you in, drinks are $4 and the rest is up to you and your pocket book.

Have fun. The **Crazy Horse** in El Dorado is similar but the atmosphere is a bit more in your face. $5 gets you in the door and beer is $5. **La Bodeguita** in Calle Uruguay always seems to have a large selection of young ladies looking to meet gringos.

Busca Panama, www.buscapanama.com, has a web site devoted to exploring this side of Panama City.

Live Music Venues

Be aware that the music scene in Panama City is a very late night thing. Some clubs do not even open before 2am, and may run wild until 8 or 9 in the morning. Clubs come and go. Hot clubs become cold and disappear with regularity.

Il Bocalino near Hooters in Calle Uruguay is known for live flamenco. **Unplugged** in the same area has a young crowd and reminds me of places I used to hang out when I was in college. **La Platea** in Casco Viejo is the spot for jazz and salsa. The **Lighthouse** in the banking district is known for local rock bands. **The Panama Social Club** in the Hotel El Panama has live jazz or salsa most nights. **La Casona de Las Brujas** is in the Casco Viejo district and features the latest in young, US-style rock.

Perhaps the best bet for the over 30 crowd who love live music is **Havana Rumba** on the Amador Causeway. Local musicians play to a mostly local crowd who are serious about listening to dedicated musicians playing the classics. This is a very good evening out if you appreciate live music in an intimate setting. *Info*: *Tel. 507-314-1197.*

Dance Clubs

Panama City has a reputation for being a hotbed of sizzling Latin dancing. **Seis**, on Calle Uruguay, is a late, late, late night dance club with just that. **Kos Panama** is next to Hooters in Calle Uruguay and features hot DJs and scorching dancing. **Acqua Bar** on Amador Causeway boasts "world famous" DJs. Could be. **Moods** in Calle Uruguay was, at the time of this writing, the trendiest dance club in town. That will probably change before you get there.

SPORTS & RECREATION

Golf

Summit Golf Club is about a 20-minute ride from the middle of Panama City and has a wonderful clubhouse and a modern, 18-hole course designed by Jeffrey Myers. The place has been around forever and is loaded with colonial-era charm. *Info: www.summitgolfpanama.com; Tel. 507-232-GOLF.*

Boating

Trips on the canal are the thing to do. Offered on Saturday only, full **canal transits** take all day while half transits take a half-day.

Attractions

Mi Pueblito is a twee tourist attraction where cheesy examples of Panamanian crafts and folklore are found. The folklore shows are littered with gringos gawking about in garish tourist outfits. Light the fuse and run. This one's a real stinker.

Birding

Panama is so chock-a-block with birds that even the heaving city has hundreds of fascinating species for birders to observe and catalogue. Twitchers arriving at the international airport for their birding trip of a lifetime have been known to leave the airport building and immediately begin birding in the parking lot before they even pick up their luggage. This is not unreasonable. Many interesting species thrive in the city.

Metropolitan Park is well within city limits and sports easy-to-see populations of parrots, toucans and manakins. Flying around among the skyscrapers and buses you can spot yellow-headed caracaras, red-legged honeycreepers, streaked saltators and orange-chinned parakeets. Remarkable.

Parks & Eco Walks

The 660-acre **Metropolitan Park** is within the city limits and is well known as a birding spot with over 220 species observed. You can expect to see both two- and three-toed sloths, squirrel monkeys and, if you are sharp-eyed, boa constrictors.

THE PANAMA CANAL

The canal area offers a wide variety of activities other than marveling at the canal itself. Thick tropical rainforest lines both sides of most of the canal. Lake Gatún and the area around Gamboa attract eco-tourists to see birds and wildlife. Fishing for peacock bass is outstanding. Amador Causeway offers visitors interesting nightlife pleasures.

SHOPPING

There are a few shops aimed at tourists in the canal area. The shop at **Miraflores Visitors Center** has the usual mix of T-shirts, molas and a couple of hats. Not very exciting.

Centro de Artesanías Internacional

Located by the YMCA in Balboa, the center has stalls with handicrafts from around Panama: carvings, molas, and other traditional crafts. This is the place to buy a Panama hat. Prices start around $20 and go on up from there. You can pay over $200 for a particularly nice, soft and pliable Panama hat. *Info: Balboa Road.*

SPORTS & RECREATION

Fishing

Lago Gatún is well known as a prime destination for landing dozens and dozens of hard fighting peacock bass. The lake is absolutely bursting with them—so many that authorities encourage catching and keeping as many as anglers can boat. Some boat well over a hundred peacock bass up to 7 lbs. per person per day. Ancon Expeditions, Tel. 507-269-9415, can arrange for half- or full-day fishing trips, usually leaving from the marina at Gamboa.

Exploring the Panama Canal

One of the best things about visiting the canal is the chance to see gigantic freighters up close. Container ships piled preposterously high with steel boxes pass within a few feet for your viewing pleasure as you stand comfortably on the shore or in the air-conditioned splendor of your tour boat.

Tours of the canal come in two flavors: half- or full-day transits. A full transit of the canal takes all day. A major part of the day is spent motoring along through Lago Gatún, which is simply not as interesting as the portion of the transit spent passing through the locks. Half-day transits focus just on the locks nearer Panama City and are usually the best bet, unless you are a retired engineer or otherwise canal-obsessed.

Another great way to see the canal and its surroundings is to take the quaint train that runs daily from Corozal to Colón daily.

Panama Marine Adventures

The *Pacific Queen* offers half-day, partial canal transits with lunch in air-conditioned splendor on Saturdays for $99. It's a 5-hour trip and includes pick up and return to Amador Causeway. Once a month they do a full transit. Call for details. *Info*: *Tel. 507-226-8917.*

Canal and Bay Tours

These guys have two boats doing both half- and full-day canal transits. They also run on Saturdays only and leave from Amador Causeway. *Info*: *Tel. 507-209-2009.*

Panama Canal Railway Company

This is a great trip. Leaving from Corozal near Balboa, the comfortable and picturesque old Canal Zone-era train leaves at 7:30am for the hour-long trip along the canal to Colón. The cars are very comfortable, and there are great, old-timey observation decks. The return trip gets into Corozal at 5:30pm. Realize that the destination town, Colón, is not a safe or interesting place for tourists. I suggest having a hired car with driver meet you at the station in Colón for a leisurely ride back to Panama City, taking in the numerous sights along the way. *Info: Tel. 507-317-6070.*

Panama Canal Rainforest Boat Adventure

Although they do not actually go through any locks, this tour takes in the wildlife around Lake Gatún with plenty of opportunity to view the huge Panamax freighters as they transit the canal. The tours leave from Gamboa and guests are picked up at their hotel and escorted through the day by a naturalist guide.

Sloths, monkeys, birds, crocs, all the expected jungle wildlife is right in your face. The awning covered boats get right up next to things. These guys really do a good job. *Info: Ancon Expeditions. www.anconexpeditions.com; Tel. 507-269-9415.*

Parks & Eco Walks

Summit

A large park/zoo, Summit is not as depressing as most zoos. Many of the cages are small and not particularly well maintained, but they have a large variety of wildlife and a stunning jaguar exhibition. The large jaguar cage contains an aging male, rescued from illegal captivity (no irony intended here). The cat stalks aggressively around his enclosure bellowing at visitors as they aim their cameras. He is really quite scary and well worth the $0.25 entry fee. The harpy eagle exhibit had two birds the last time I was there and they were a bit hard to see.

This is a good spot to get close to local animals and birds so you can get some great, up-close photos. You don't have to tell anyone back home you took the shots at the zoo.

Gamboa

On the banks of the Chagres River and the canal, Gamboa is a small, former Canal Zone residential town that has been converted into a large, luxury ecolodge and center for tourism. The lodge (see *Best Sleeps & Eats* chapter) is large and fairly upscale. They have an excellent serpentarium (snake house), orchid house, butterfly garden and lots of walks by the lake. It is a birding hot spot. The Lagarto Restaurant is agreeably located on the banks of the river but the food is unremarkable (unmentionable at times).

Soberanía National Park

The 55,000-acre park runs along the east side of the Panama Canal and consists of mountainous tropical rainforest. It is close to Panama City, and has well developed trails and two resorts bordering it. Gamboa Lodge is an upscale resort on Lake Gatún. Canopy Tower is a basic birders' lodge with world-class guides. The famous birding site Pipeline Road is within the park. **More than 400 bird species** have been encountered in the 54,000-acre park.

There are several roads and trails that can be appreciated by even a casual visitor. You can actually take a bus or cab to get here from Panama City, enjoy the park for a day and return home in the evening the same way with plenty of time left over for a night on the town. Birders will be looking for antshrikes, manakins, tanagers and rufous motmots.

Monkey Island

Someone marooned a few capuchin monkeys on a small island along the side of the Panama Canal. There are now 15 of them; 14 males and 1 female. Most of the males are her sons. The alpha male claims the female (as one does). You can't help but feel sorry for the poor sons.

Birding

Birding in the canal area is exceptional by any standard. It includes several of the top birding destinations in the world. Top-quality guides are available who can satisfy even the most experienced birders.

Canopy Tower

This bird-oriented lodge hosts enthusiastic and experienced birders from all over the world. The lodge itself is a remodeled radar tower rising through the rainforest canopy, providing a unique view for guests and visitors. They employ some of the most dedicated and knowledgeable guides anywhere. All the hotspots are very close.

Pipeline Road

With a list exceeding 400 species, this overgrown maintenance road is the best place in the world to see tropical forest bird species. You can drive along some of it, but walking very early in the morning is the holiest way to behave on Pipeline Road. With luck, you might see a sapayoa, buff-rumped warbler, dull-mantled antbird or even a crake.

Ammo Dump

If you simply must add a crake to your life list, Ammo Dump is a likely spot. Park near the gates and wander quietly around the banks of the pond. If you must, call them with your iPod. The crakes are here.

BOCAS DEL TORO

Bocas is a rapidly growing tourist town **aimed squarely at younger travelers.** A thumping reggae vibe hangs over the place. Bars and tour companies crowd out backpacker hostels and hotels on the main street though town. The whole place seems to be built over the water on stilts. Even the fire department is on the water with a large deck over the bay. Firemen lounge about listening to blaring reggaeton. Looks more like a bar than a *bombero* (fire house).

SHOPPING

There are a few places to buy beachwear, hats and stuff and a few scruffy types selling beads at the square, but it's not really a shopping destination.

Super Gourmet

Serving mostly the large expat community, this shop has a real delicatessen, wine and booze as well as organic products. *Info*: *Next to Hotel Bahía. Tel. 507-757-9357.*

Casa Azul

Artisan-produced gifts and "home accessories" make up the stock. *Info*: *Next to Starfish Coffee. Tel. 507-757-9357.*

NIGHTLIFE & ENTERTAINMENT

Nightlife and entertainment are what Bocas Town is all about. The place heaves with bars and loud music emporiums every night until past dawn. The hottest, trendiest spots change, so check with your lodge or hotel for recommendations about the newest and best place to get smashed. Getting smashed is pretty much what it's all about. Avoid watermelon mojitos.

Baumfaulk's

Not a gay bar, Bum Fuck's – as everyone calls it – is named after its colorful owner Bill Baumfaulk. The usual crowd includes visiting and local gringos mixed with a few young locals looking for gringo friends. It's loud, it's cool. It's great. *Info*: *Near the park.*

Barco Hundido

Apparently, the original bar sank at the dock, so they just opened a new one above it on pilings. The place rocks. Most of the action starts after midnight. It's built on and over the water with a large, floating bar on some sort of barge that has its own outboard motor. Reportedly, the owner gets into things himself from time to time and quietly unhooks the barge/bar from the dock and takes revelers off into the islands on an impromptu booze cruise. Don't worry if this happens to you—there is a bar on board. Without a doubt, this is the loudest place in town, rocking from 10pm until 5am or later. They occasionally have live bands. *Info: Calle 1.*

SPORTS & RECREATION

Diving & Snorkeling

While not a first-class scuba diving destination, Bocas has excellent snorkeling. **Parque Nacional Marino Isla Bastamientos** is a standout. Don't miss a snorkeling/beachcombing trip to Cayos Zapatillas. The small, picturesque islets are surrounded with good snorkeling.

You'll see tourists jumping into the water and splashing about in front of the seaside bars and hotels. Several have slides and other water toys to facilitate this. Realize that all of the hundred or so bars, restaurants and other businesses fronting the water pipe their waste streams (toilets) directly into this same, seemingly inviting sea. Gross.

Jampan Tours

For snorkeling trips, I suggest the shorter $17 trip. For another $5 you get to go to the national park around Zapatilla Island. The snorkeling is not quite as good as on the shorter, cheaper trip to Crawl Cay. Many people have to go to Zapatilla, since one of the *Survivor* TV series was filmed there. It's not that exciting. *Info: Tel. 507-757-9619.*

Bocas Water Sports

For hard-core divers, Bocas Water Sports offers full PADI services. The have two and three tank dives with all the usual rental equipment. *Info: www.bocaswatersports.com; Tel. 507-757-9541.*

Fishing

Trolling for tuna from local dugouts or small outboards can be productive. The best time for tuna is March, April and May. Most of the time anglers can expect to nail a kingfish or two, a couple of snapper and some jack or needlefish. Tarpon, snook and other interesting game fish are in the area but the fishery has not been explored or developed for visitors to enjoy. There are no proper charter boats working in the Bocas area.

Jampan Tours

Jampan offers fishing in local boats. This usually involves trolling with deep-diving Rapalas or local dead bait for kingfish, barracuda, and, possibly, a nice snapper. *Info*: *Tel. 507-757-9619.*

Golf
Red Frog Beach Resort has an Arnold Palmer-designed 18-holer.

Boating
Jampan Tours
Jampan has a variety of houseboats and other medium-sized craft available for multi-day cruises through the archipelago. This is a great way to see the area. The boats come all set up with cooking facilities, bedding and snorkeling gear. *Info: Tel. 507-757-9619.*

Kayaking
Bocas is a wonderful area for kayaking. There is always just one more tropical isle off in the distance that needs to be explored. The area around Bocas town teems with boat traffic and wakes can be a problem. The best kayaking is far from town. Many of the lodges have kayaks for guest use. If you can, try to arrange to get to the Zapatillas or Swan Cay, where the water and scenery are superb.

Bocas Water Sports
Bocas Water Sports rents both one-person and two-person, sit-on kayaks for half or full day rental. Their location is close to some good areas for exploration. *Info: www.bocaswatersports.comTel. 507-757-9541.*

Surfing
Bocas is the top surf destination in Panama. There may be better waves elsewhere but Bocas has all the other stuff surfers love: cheap eats, cheap sleeps and rowdy nightspots booming out DJ sounds. The best waves generally arrive from December through March, although nearby storms can kick things up nicely from time to time.

Red Frog Beach is perhaps the most famous spot, but The Dumps, Playa Punch and Playa Primera offer waves to challenge jaded surfers. You can rent surfboards in town from a small shack near the park.

Birding

Isla Escudo de Veraguas in the Bocas del Toro archipelago is the only place on the planet where you can find the tiny Escudo hummingbird. In Panama, you'll only find the elusive stub-tailed spadebill in these islands. Three-wattled bellbirds and Montezuma oropendolas are also attractions for birders. Swan Cay, *Isla Pájaros,* hosts the only Caribbean breeding colony of the red-billed tropicbird. Nearby **San San Pond Sack** wetlands are a major draw for birders. Ancon Expeditions at the Bocas Inn can set you up with area guides.

Beaches, Parks & Eco Walks

Parque Nacional Marino Isla Bastamientos protects large areas of Isla Bastamientos and the nearby underwater reefs. Some snorkeling spots are marked and have buoys for tying boats.

Cayos Zapatillas are cool little beach islands all by themselves with no one on them but you and your fellow tourists. These two tiny islets are picture postcard perfect with white sand and a few palm trees. This is a good spot for a picnic or romantic interlude.

There are several nice beaches in Bocas del Toro. Playa La Cabana, Big Creek, Red Frog and Playa Bluff are perhaps the best. Some are good for swimming and others for surfing. Watch out for undertow and tiderips where the surf is high.

SAN BLAS ARCHIPELAGO

The San Blas Archipelago, more formally known as the **Kuna Yala**, is one of the most picturesque groups of islands in the world. White sand, clear blue water, waving palm trees, colorful natives—San Blas seemingly has it all. The only drawbacks are that the area is quite hard to get to, and there are no tourist facilities except of the most basic type. Fortunately, there is a luxury lodge close by that offers trips and tours into the beautiful area.

The Kuna are very particular about allowing visitors into their province, and expect to be paid for every visitor, and ask for a small fee for a visit to any island. Even real tiny ones. Every coconut tree and the coconuts that fall from them are owned by a local Indian. They rely on trading coconuts with the Colombians for staples.

The Kuna can also be very particular about photographs. They expect $1 per shot of any individual. Photos of villages in general usually go for around $5. If you bring a video camera to a Kuna island, expect to pay as much as $50 for the privilege.

SHOPPING

There is no commercial infrastructure in the area—no restaurants, no hotels, no shops except for a couple of very, very basic, native-run places. The only things in the area to buy are wonderful fabrics sewn by local Kuna Indian women. Women approach visitors full-on with *molas* for sale. You can't avoid them. Prices run from $5 to over $100 per panel, depending on complexity and authenticity.

The women rarely bargain unless you are buying several *molas*. See *Best Activities*, Panama City for information about Flory Saltzman's mola shop. She has been buying from the Kunas for decades, and has a huge selection at prices usually at least as good as you can get from the Kuna women yourself.

SPORTS & RECREATION

Snorkeling

The Kunas do not allow any scuba diving in their waters but the snorkeling can be good. Small out islands can be good spots with coral reefs chock-a-block with colorful fish. I suggest you refrain for snorkeling near any Kuna settlement, because they discharge all waste directly into the waters around their homes. Not healthy for swimmers.

Good scuba diving is to be had for guests at luxurious **Coral Lodge** (see *Best Sleeps*). The lodge is located at the border of the Kuna Yala Province and there are good, reasonably unfished reefs just offshore.

San Blas Adventures
Elias Perez can arrange for snorkeling trips in pangas. He speaks quite good English and is outgoing and cheerful. *Info: Corbisky Island. Tel. 507-6708-5254.*

Fishing

Kuna Indians do a good job of hoovering the seas around them and sucking up anything edible. As a result, fishing in the area is only fair. Trolling for kingfish, snapper and needlefish is about the only possible fishing activity. Don't expect to catch anything of any size. Unfortunately, the local noble Indians have a reputation for using bleach and other chemicals to flush lobster, squid, crab and other edibles out of their reef nooks and crannies into their awaiting nets.

San Blas Adventures
Elias Perez can arrange for fishing trips to the San Blas in pangas. He speaks quite good English and is outgoing and cheerful. *Info: Corbisky Island. Tel. 507-6708-5254.*

Boating

The archipelago can only be appreciated properly by boat—that's how the locals get around. The islands cover many square miles and, if you want to see how the Indians live traditionally on the out islands, you'll need to get a tour by boat. You simply must get around these beautiful islands in a boat to appreciate the area.

Few of the water taxis or other boats you are likely to take in the Kuna Yala are equipped with life jackets. Most have no anchors, paddles, radios or other safety equipment. If safety helmets, rear-facing child seats, and other protective equipment is important to you—don't come here. This is third world Indian country. They just don't do things the same way you are used to.

San Blas Adventures
Helpful Elias Perez arranges all types of excursions around the San Blas in pangas. He speaks quite good English and is outgoing and cheerful. *Info: Corbisky Island, Tel. 507-6708-5254.*

Birding

The San Blas islands have a comparatively low density of bird species compared to other parts of Panama. The Kuna Yala mainland is, for all practical purposes, inaccessible and has not really been explored thoroughly by birders. There are no qualified local guides, although nationally recognized bird guides can help more adventurous groups navigate in the area.

The **mangroves** and **offshore islands** of San Blas are home to numerous species, including anhingas, bare-throated tiger herons, wood storks and yellow-crowned night herons.

Beaches, Parks & Eco Walks

It's hard to imagine more picturesque beaches and stunning, picture postcard tropical isles. White sand, clear water, palm trees heavy with coconuts—they're all here. Keep in mind that every island in the area is owned by someone, and most want to charge a fee for visitors. Usually it's a mere $1 per person, so it would be unkind to object. The Indians can be forgiven for trying to extract some money from the passing tourist hordes.

Kayaking

If you are really into kayaking and don't mind a little camping, consider an island hopping holiday with sea kayaks. You can spend a few days or a few weeks traveling around the cays sleeping in native huts or on the sand. This would be a beautiful expedition, but is only for the hardy. Kayaking around Coral Lodge is excellent. There are miles and miles of mangroves to explore and nearby coral reefs to snorkel. It's a beautiful area.

What is Ecotourism, Anyway?

Ecotourism is a term that you'll hear kicked around quite a bit on your travels in Panama. Of course, most visitors to the area are here to enjoy the natural wonders, but does that make us all ecotourists? Does spending a couple of hours strolling through the forest with a herd of other tourists make you an ecotourist? Or must you spend a week helping the students with their research at some remote biological station to earn the title?

In fact, ecotourism is a state of mind, an ideal of sustainable, minimally invasive tourism that both visitors and those in the tourism industry should strive for (alas, both groups often fall far short of the ideal). Ecotourists leave no litter, don't feed or interfere with the animals, and consume nothing but products that are harvested in a sustainable manner. A true ecolodge recycles and conserves, releases no waste into the environment, strives to use renewable energy, and generally tries to have as little impact on the natural habitat as possible.

Ecotourism is also about preserving a very important species called local workers. One of the central concepts of ecotourism is the idea that local people can make a better living by helping tourists enjoy the rain forest than they could by chopping it down. Good ecotourists patronize local businesses, and buy local products whenever possible. The International Ecotourism Society, *www.ecotourism.org*, includes lists of enviro-friendly lodges and tour operators.

Aventuras Panamá
All specialized gear, guides, kayaks and camping equipment is provided on four and five-day sea kayak adventures. *Info*: *www.aventuraspanama.com; Tel. 507-260-0044.*

GULF OF CHIRIQUÍ

The focus for visitors to the Gulf is on the sea. There is no tourist-oriented shopping or nightlife. It is difficult to visit the area unless you stay in one of the all-inclusive fishing or luxury lodges, but it's well worth the trouble.

SPORTS & RECREATION

Diving & Snorkeling

The best diving in Panama is found in the waters around Isla Coiba. Diving in the Central American Pacific does not involve extensive coral reefs and crystal clear water such as one can encounter in the Caribbean. The water is so chock full of plankton that visibility is relatively low, but the rich soup means incredibly rich sea life. Fish are all over the place.

Due to nearby deep water and plenty of food to eat, divers can expect to see deep-water pelagics like tuna, amberjack and possibly sailfish or marlin. Huge manta rays follow divers about like dogs wanting to play. A variety of whales use the Gulf for breeding and raising their young. On a recent dive near Coiba Island Marine Park, a small humpback swam directly under me and turned its head for a look at me. Cool!

The coast is mostly lined with mangroves and there are few towns or villages. Most visitors either stay on one of the remote lodges or on one of the liveaboard dive or fishing boats. Access is either by flying into David and taking a boat from nearby

Pedregal or by flying directly into the small dirt strip at Islas Secas Lodge.

Fishing

Some of the best fishing in the world is available at famous hot spots like Hannibal Bank. Less famous but perhaps more productive are Isla Montuoso or Islas Ladrones. Sailfish, marlin, dorado, yellowfin tuna, huge snapper and wahoo are the local targets.

Pesca Panama

Based in Pedregal, near David, Pesca Panama is a mother boat operation. A large, comfortable barge has been fitted out for 14 guests. Anglers are taken to remote fishing grounds where the mother ship anchors for several days while anglers fish from 27' center consoles. The operation is professional, the accommodations are comfortable and the food is good. The fishing is outstanding. This is a good option for hardcore anglers. *Info: Boca Chica. www.pescapanama.com; Tel. 800-946-3474, 507-6614-5850.*

Panama Big Game Sport Fishing Club

On remote Boca Brava Island, Panama Big Game hosts up to 8 anglers in relative luxury. Air-conditioned rooms, wonderful food and drink

make for comfortable evenings after spending the day trolling on one of the lodge's three boats, including a Bertram 31.This is a pro operation. A group of fishermen I accompanied recently spent four days fishing and ended up with a marlin apiece and dozens of tuna and dorado. Wahoo were so numerous we declared them to be a menace. See *Best Sleeps* for more information. *Info*: Boca Brava Island. *Tel. 507-6627-5431, 786-600-1672 US.* www.panama-sportfishing.com.

Coiba Adventure

American Capt. Tom Yust has been running fishing charters in the

Panama area for over 15 years. His Coiba Island-based operation can handle up to 8 anglers. Their best boat is a restored Bertram 31' with all the goodies. Accommodations are air-conditioned and comfortable. The fishing is superb. *Info: Tel. 507-999-8108, 800-800-0907. www.coibadventure.com.*

Whale Watching

The Gulf of Chiriquí is simply stuffed with whales. Every time I have been on the water there I have seen whales breaching, doing head stands and generally disporting themselves aggressively for tourists. Whale researchers (based at Islas Secas Resort) believe the whales use the area for breeding and raising their young. Humpbacks, sperm and false killer whales abound. The best way to see them is to stay at **Islas Secas Resort** or on **Coiba Island** and take small boats out exploring for them.

Birding

The Gulf of Chiriquí is fringed with miles and miles of mangroves making a home for several wading bird species. Expect to see black-bellied whistling duck, roseate spoonbill, black-hooded antshrike and tropical peewee. Whimbrels, dowitchers and willets are particularly well represented in the area.

The wild islands in the gulf are nesting sites for pelagics. Birders will appreciate brown boobies, sandwich terns, magnificent frigate birds, and anhingas.

Surfing

The Gulf of Chiriquí boasts a couple of the top surfing spots in the world. From Punta Burica, near the border with Costa Rica, to Coiba Island there are dozens of hot spots, but the ones most surfers go on about are Las Lajas and Morro Negrito.

Morro Negrito Surf Camp is located on its own small island with great breaks directly in front of the lodging. All you need to bring is your trunks and perhaps shoes. They supply everything else and have boats for fishing or for visiting remote reef breaks. This is about as good as it gets for surfing vacations. *Info: www.surferparadise.com.*

THE CENTRAL HIGHLANDS

Spectacular mountain valleys, volcanoes and cloud forests lure visitors to Boquete and El Valle. Beaches are just icing on the cake. Birders and sun worshippers flock to the highlands and beaches. Hiking, surfing, white-water rafting and observing wildlife top the list of things to do.

SHOPPING

Although there are a variety of tourist-oriented items for sale, the **wonderful Panamanian coffee** is really the only thing worth purchasing while you are in the area. **Boquete** in particular is a famous coffee-producing region. Some of the best and most expensive coffees in the world are produced on the slopes of Volcán Barú.

Café Ruiz

Featuring their own locally-produced products, this roadside shop is the starting and ending point for the company's tour of their nearby farm, *beneficio* and roasting operation. Wonderful, fresh roasted coffee is for sale for immediate consumption or for the road. Various roasts are available as well as examples of some of the more interesting local heirloom *típico* varieties. Ask for some geisha, currently the trendiest of coffee varieties. *Info: Center of Bajo Boquete. Tel. 507-720-1000.*

NIGHTLIFE & ENTERTAINMENT

This is not an area for nightlife other than a decent **casino** in David. Observing wildlife, drinking coffee, retiring and hiking are what most visitors do. Most go to bed early to be ready for the 6am bird walk.

SPORTS & RECREATION

Golf

The all-inclusive Decameron has an adequate 18-hole course within sight of the beach. *Info: www.decameron.com; Tel. 507-215-5000.*

Hiking

With nearby Volcán Barú, mountain hiking simply doesn't get much better. A number of ancient Indian trails are still serviceable and are still in use by local Indians. Quetzal searches are one of the most popular ways to see the cloud forest and, hopefully, this very colorful bird that is the end-all and be-all for many birders.

Coffee Adventures

Hans & Terry van der Vooren lead groups on a variety of highland tours including bird trips, coffee farm visits and trips to see a Ngöbe Buglé Indian village. They lead groups in English, Spanish, Dutch and German. *Info: Boquete. Tel. 507-720-3852.*

Rafting

The Chiriquí Viejo, Rió Grande and Chagres Rivers offer everything from quiet floats to class IV and V rapids. Outfitters haul punters in vans to put in sites, usually a couple of hours away from lodging. Be sure to ask about river levels if there has been lots of rain.

Aventuras Panamá

Several different trips for different levels of rafters are offered. *Info: Tel. 507-260-0044.*

Attractions

Canopy Adventure

For $40 you get to zip through the jungle and over waterfalls over 100 feet up in the air. The runs are not particularly steep. The area is perfect for wildlife viewing, especially birds, after everyone stops screaming from the zip line adrenaline rush. They are located just up the road from Canopy Lodge. *Info: El Valle. Tel. 507-264-5720.*

Birding

Quetzals, trogons and three-wattled bellbirds lead the show in the cloud-forested mountains around Boquete. One of the top birding tours in Panama takes in Altos de Maria, a new, gigantic housing development that has plenty of open area along side almost virgin forest, allowing unusual viewing opportunities. Expect to encounter purplish-backed quail-doves, purple-throated trogons, brown-billed scythebills and, of course, black-crowned antpittas.

Canopy Lodge high above El Valle is a sister to the famous Canopy Tower and is, likewise, a haven for hard-core birders. They flock here for possible sightings of rufous-vented ground-cuckoo.

Boquete has a population of dedicated and knowledgeable bird guides. Hans van der Voorens is a good choice. Nearby Barú Volcano Park is one of the favorite areas for bird expeditions.

DARIEN

Vast, unexplored or unexplorable **jungle covered-mountains** and **impenetrable swamps** make up Darien Province. There are few towns, almost no roads and only a few isolated jungle airstrips. All this isolation and difficulty of access makes the Darien one of the few truly wild places left on the planet, and a top draw for ecotourists and birders. Visitors to Darien should be ready for a little bit of **roughing it**.

SPORTS & RECREATION

Diving & Snorkeling

Although Darien has a long Pacific coast, very little diving or snorkeling is done. There are virtually no facilities of any kind until you get to the Colombian border, except for the luxury-fishing lodge Tropic Star in Piñas Bay. Except for in the Pearl Islands, there are no organized dive operators. Undoubtedly, there is **wonderful diving** to be found around the rocks and seamounts of this wild coast. So far, **only a few of the more adventurous** have taken the time to explore the underwater world of Darien.

Diving and snorkeling around the Pearl Islands, just offshore from the Darien, is an option. Big sharks, manta rays and possibly pelagics are seen on trips from Contadora Island and Isla San José. There are a few lodges and one luxury hotel in the islands.

Aquatic Sport Center

Operating out of the Hotel Contadora, the company offers sightseeing trips around the islands, scuba and snorkeling expeditions. The diving can be very good. *Info: Hotel Contadora. Tel. 507-250-4186.*

Fishing

"Panama" is an Indian word meaning "an abundance of fish." Say no more. Although the Darien area is famous for impenetrable jungles and swamps, it also happens to have what is without doubt the top fishing lodge in the world. Tropic Star Lodge hosts up to 35 anglers in true luxury. Fine dining, air-conditioned rooms and true top shelf service are difficult to accomplish miles from anywhere in *National Geographic* country, but Tropic Star manages. Everything is brought in from Panama City by plane or supply boat. Fishing is done on immaculately maintained, classic **31' Bertrams**. Captains and mates train for years or even decades to earn their coveted positions.

I have fished at the top fishing lodges in Central America and the Caribbean, and can confidently say that Tropic Star offers the best fishing for billfish and other tropical species. The lodge is almost always full. You need to book as much as a year in advance to be sure of having a place. Celebrities flock there for the luxury atmosphere and world-class fishing. Management will not let me repeat the names of the famous and mighty who frequent this very well-run lodge. *Info: Bahía Piñas. www.tropicstar.com; Tel. 507-250-4186.*

Birding

The **harpy eagle**, crested eagle, golden-headed quetzal and several types of macaws draw sharp-eyed birders from around the planet.

Famous the world over for extravagant birding, the Darien is difficult to get to, and few birders venture to sites other than the wonderful **Cana** and **Punta Patiño**. Both of these sites can be visited through the highly efficient Ancon Expeditions. Punta Patiño is famous for sightings of **black oropendolas** (*see next page*) and Cana is the place to go for a **great curassow** or a choco tapaculo.

Tropic Star Lodge in Piñas Bay is perhaps the most luxurious and famous fishing lodge in the world. Guests are 100% focused on catch and release **fishing for billfish**. Birders who visit can expect to see great green macaws, tody motmots and puffbirds. White-fronted nunbirds are the stars in the area.

If you go offshore, **magnificent pelagics** perform their acrobatics for you. Expect to see brown boobies, brown noddys and wedge-rumped storm petrels. The lodge has naturalist guides and forest rangers but no trained bird guides.

Of course the most famous of the feathered inhabitants of Darien is the **harpy eagle**. This mighty bird is known to jump down and haul off monkeys, sloths and other small furry creatures to devour in their nests at leisure. Hard-core birders hope to view them on their nest with the young ones **tearing dead things into shreds** and swallowing them. Quite a show.

Although just outside Darien Province, the lovely **Pearl Islands** offer the only place in Panama to see the white-fringed antwren, a singular LBB (Little Brown Bird).

Beaches, Parks & Eco Walks

Other than **Tropic Star Lodge** in Bahía Piñas, there are only a couple of places in the Darien you can actually go. While it is possible to drive from Panama City along Route 1 to Yaviza, there is little point in doing so. The route is lined with cattle pastures cleared from the forest now supplying low-grade beef to American fast food restaurants. Once you get to Yaviza, a crummy end-of-the-road town, there is no place else to go and not much of interest to do.

The best way to see the Darien is to fly to one of **Ancon Expeditions** jungle camps or go on one of their cross Darien treks. Neither option is for those who insist on air-conditioning and chocolates on their pillows. The camps are "comfortable" enough, and are good bases for doing what is best to do in the Darien: observing the plentiful wildlife, especially the birds.

Don't go on one of these Darien trips with Ancon unless you have at least **a strong passion for birds.** Almost all of the guests are hard-core birders and talk obsessively about almost nothing else. Fine with me—I like to listen to them.

Cana Field Station is one of the top birding destinations in the world. Ancon provides rustic accommodations (hot showers) and top guides. Trips to Cana are either five or eight days long and are always accompanied by a top naturalist guide. Visitors are flown into the **remote airstrip** on charter flights.

Punta Patiño is on the Pacific coast, so you are exposed to both lowland and upland species. The lodging is perhaps a little more comfortable than Cana. You have hot water and private baths. Food is served family-style in the large dining room with spectacular views out to sea and over the jungled hills. This is **harpy eagle country** and birders flock here to observe them on their nests. *Info: Ancon Expeditions, www.anconexpeditions.com; Tel. 507-269-9515.*

The ultimate Darien experience is to trek all the way across the isthmus from the Caribbean to the Pacific. Once again, **Ancon Expeditions** is the company to set you on your way. They custom design treks for the hardy. All transportation, food and equipment can be arranged. The trips involve lots of walking and trips along remote jungle rivers in native dugouts. Nights are sometimes spent in **Embera Indian villages**, giving punters a true taste of Indian life in the Darien (and where you can buy some beautiful baskets and other crafts – *see photo below*). The trips usually take 14 days. Darien adventure doesn't get any better than this.

13. PRACTICAL MATTERS

GETTING TO PANAMA

By Air

Tocumen International Airport (PTY) is the big one just outside town. Virtually all of the international flights arrive there. It's fairly new and modern, loaded with glitterati-type duty free shops. Flights within Panama almost all leave from Albrook—on the other side of town. There is a $20 international departure tax to be paid at the airport upon departure. Of course, be sure your ticket is to Panama City, *Panama* (PTY) and not Panama City, Florida (PFN), also a nice place.

Albrook (PAC) is what everyone calls Aeropuerto Marcos A. Gelabert. It's in the former Canal Zone part of town—on the other side of Panama City from Tocumen International Airport. Albrook is where almost all of the internal, Panamanian flights originate. Both Aeroperlas and Air Panama do their thing at Albrook. Pay no attention to the departure and arrival signs in the waiting areas; ask. They seem to leave the same old, out-of-date signs up all the time.

By Cruise

Numerous cruise lines target Panama. Trips through the Canal are heaven for a serious cruiser. Some lines stop for a day in Bocas del Toro, the San Blas and other, out-of-the-way destinations.

Celebrity Cruise Line
Ships leave from Fort Lauderdale and San Francisco. *Info: Tel. 800-722-5941; www.celebrity.com.*

Norwegian Cruise Line
Nice ships leave from Miami and Los Angeles. *Info: Tel. 866-234-7350; www.ncl.com.*

Regent Seven Seas Cruises
Regent (formerly Radisson) is the Rolls Royce of cruise lines. Their 14 and 16 night cruises leave from Ft. Lauderdale and San Francisco. Some trips include Los Angeles. *Info: Tel. 954-776-6123; www.rssc.com.*

Zegrahm Expeditions
Zegrahm offers an eco-oriented itinerary aboard the 80-passenger Levant that includes Belize, Honduras, Costa Rica, and Panama. *Info: Tel. 800-628-8747; www.zeco.com.*

GETTING AROUND PANAMA

By Air
Panama has two almost indistinguishable local airlines: **Aeroperlas** and **Air Panama**. They operate mostly 21-seat Twin Otters and fly out of the domestic airport, *Aeropuerto Marcos A. Gelabert*, known by almost everyone as "Albrook." Some of the planes are a little on the creaky side and are definitely not up to high US standards, but accidents are rare. I have been in several where I could see light around the edges of the door and feel a draft after taking off. This was fine since the AC didn't work very well anyway. *Info: Aeroperlas – Tel. 507-315-7500; www.aeroperlas.com. Air Panama – Tel. 507-316-9000; www.flyairpanama.com.*

Some remote lodges are accessible only by landing on short, dirt runways in jungle clearings. This is part of why they call it "adventure travel."

By Boat
Remote lodges along both coasts often use small water taxis or fiberglass boats to bring guests to and from the mainland. Usually this is fine. Most of the boats have awnings, and seas are usually calm. However, especially in the San Blas area, much of this type of transportation takes place in small, beat up, leaky boats with

dodgy-looking outboards. Lifejackets are not always available. Sometimes little attempt is made to keep luggage dry. You are very likely to get at least some spray and, from time to time, you can get absolutely drenched.

I have traveled to some lodges in boats with no paddles, anchors, life preservers or radios. Avoid the San Blas area if this bothers you.

By Car / Car Rental

The best way to enjoy a short stay in Panama City is to hire an English-speaking driver. You can hire almost any cab in town for $10 an hour, but most drivers speak only fair English, if any. I suggest you call **José**, who will arrange for local drivers with excellent English. He gets $12 an hour but it's worth it. I've used several of his drivers to haul me around town and even out into the country some. José also offers airport pick-ups for two people at $25. Not bad.

Talk & Drive?

As in most of the world, **it's against the law in Panama to drive and talk on a cell phone** at the same time. Not a bad idea.

I've used several of his drivers and had a great time with them. Their English was very good and they took me to all sorts of places I would never thought of on my own (including a drive by ex-strongman Noriega's house). It's cheaper and much less hassle than renting a car. *Info: Panama City. Tel. 507-6614-7811.*

It is not possible to take cars rented in Panama into Costa Rica or otherwise out of the country. Some agencies insist that all drivers be at least 25 years old. Extra collision insurance is required and some companies will not accept your US insurance. Rental car coverage provided by credit cards is not always accepted.

There are several car rental counters at the international and domestic airports in Panama City. The airport in David also has several.

- **Hertz**, *Tel. 507-263-6511; www.hertz.com.pa*
- **Alamo**, *Tel. 507-236-5777; www.alamopanama.com*

By Taxi

Taxis in Panama are cheap, cheap, cheap. You can go almost anywhere within most cities for $2. With a little bargaining, you can rent cabs for $8 to $10 an hour. As you should do anywhere, always ask the price before getting into the cab. There is usually little or no haggling. Resist the urge to tip. It's just not done in Panama, and fares are usually an exact dollar amount: $1 or $2 so you won't be tempted to round up.

There are zillions of taxis zooming around and you will find them honking at you more or less annoyingly as you walk around. Sharing taxi rides with strangers is common. Just because a cab appears to have a fare already doesn't mean you should not try to flag it down. Not all are air-conditioned.

Tourist taxis, with "SET" license plates, are usually parked in front of the better hotels and often charge three or four times the rate of ordinary ones. You can usually just walk out to the street and flag down a regular old cab and save some money.

Most of the big tourist hotels allow only the SET (expensive tourist taxis) to wait in front and are reluctant to hunt you up a regular taxi. Recently, I wanted to go from my hotel just outside town into Panama City, about a 10-minute ride. The hotel doorman efficiently snatched my bags and placed them inside a waiting cab. When I asked, I was told the price would be $20. When I demurred, removed my bags from the cab, and asked about a regular cab, all the porters and the doorman melted away. I walked a couple of hundred feet to the main road, flagged down a passing cab and shared a ride into town. The price? $1.75.

By Bus

Colorful and cheap, converted school buses seem to be everywhere. You just flag them down or wait at a marked bus stop. You pay when you get off. These *diablos rojos* (red devils) are almost always jam-packed, are not air-conditioned, and are not really practical if you have much luggage.

The **modern bus station in Panama City** is located across the street from Albrook Mall, right by the Albrook airport. You can get long-distance buses here for destinations all over the country. These buses tend to be modern, air-conditioned and relatively comfortable. They also tend to be jam-packed with many people standing in the crowded aisles. Their radios, tuned to mind-numbing pop stations, are usually cranked up to ear-splitting volume. Luggage can be put on the roof rack. The long-distance buses are efficient, cheap and fast. Most destinations within the country are less than $5.

BASIC INFORMATION

Banking & Changing Money

Panama uses US dollars although change may come occasionally in local coins called **Balboas**. This makes financial transactions easy. There is no need to change money—ATMs are the best way to get cash.

In general, banks are slow and bureaucratic nightmares. Avoid them if possible. Since there is no need to actually change your US dollars into local currency, there is little need to use them. ATMs usually offer the best exchange rate, even after the credit card clearing companies take a small slice of the action. If you do need the services of a bank, branch offices at Albrook Mall, the bus station or Multiplaza Mall are convenient and you may not have to wait as long as at main branches in town.

Major credit cards are accepted widely but be sure to ask in advance if you are visiting more remote areas. Some local restaurants and other businesses work with cash only.

Business Hours

Panama operates to US standards for working hours. Commercial entities open around 8 or 9 and close around 5 or 6.

Restaurants generally start serving lunch around 12 and dinner around six, but don't be surprised if no one else but you arrives until after 9 or so. Many bars and clubs don't get going or even open their doors until well after midnight. Call first.

Climate & Weather
Even though it is close to the equator, Panama enjoys a relatively temperate climate.

Temperatures rarely get above 80° F in the daytime or below 70 at night, as much of the country is at relatively high, cool altitude or subject to cooling trade winds. Even so, it can get quite humid and you can soak a shirt through with sweat walking around Panama City on a summer afternoon. You probably won't need a jacket of any sort unless you plan long jungle treks through high altitude cloud forests.

Rain is part of the fun. Rainy season runs more or less from May to December but conditions vary quite a bit due to local circumstances. Tropical downpours can be intense but rarely last long. Weeks and weeks of steady rain are not normal. Short, intense, afternoon rainsqualls are the norm. They usually just serve to cool things down a bit.

It doesn't make much sense to plan a trip based on avoiding rain. There are several Panamanian microclimates that may mean more or less rain than is usual across the country for the time you plan on visiting. It may be raining intensely in Bocas while David suffers a dry spell.

Consulates & Embassies
Panama City is a thriving international hub for business, and sports embassies and consulates from over 150 countries.

The **United States Embassy** is a biggie. *Info: Avenida Balboa, Calles 37 & 38. Tel. 507-207-7000.*

Electricity
Electric current and fixtures in Panama are the same as in the US. Plugs are usually two-prong and not grounded. Remote lodges may run on generators or solar power. Some may turn the power off at night. This

means you may not be able to run your laptop or hairdryer whenever you like.

Emergencies & Safety

Panama doesn't have a proper 911 service, but you can call a private ambulance. *Info: Tel. 507-269-9778.*

Crime

As in any country, you need to take care of yourself. There are thieves preying on the unwary all over the world and Panama is no different. While Panama City is relatively safe, **Colón** suffers a harsh reputation for street crime. Just don't go there. There is nothing of interest there anyway.

Few visitors have any problem with crime, but it is a good idea to keep copies of your passport and an extra credit card separate from the rest of your luggage. Use the in room safes provided by most hotels. Don't take up with strangers you meet on the street.

I have heard only a couple of reports of tourists being targeted with "date rape drugs," but it can happen anywhere, so never leave your drinks unattended in a bar or restaurant while you visit the loo.

If you mess around with any of the women you might meet at Panama City casinos or nightclubs, you should use appropriate caution. Don't take all of your money with you on such excursions. If you bring dubious ladies back to your room, be sure to leave the bulk of your valuables in the safe or in a friend's room. These women know to look under the mattress for your stash.

Health & Hospitals

You do not need any special inoculations or shots before visiting Panama. In almost all cases, you can drink water right out of the tap with no worries. Malaria is pretty much a thing of the past but, if you plan on spending more than a month or so in remote areas like Darien, it would be a good idea to take prophylactic pills.

Panama is famous for **top-quality health care at bargain prices**. Many visitors come to Panama for medical reasons. There is an excellent, modern hospital in Panama City. Others are not as up-to-date, although the hospital in David is considered to be excellent as well. **Punta Pacifica** is affiliated with Johns Hopkins. *Info: Blvd. Pacifica. Tel. 507-204-8000. www.hospitalpuntapacifica.com.*

Etiquette

In general, Panamanians pay more attention to the social niceties than do Americans. It is important to say at least "*buenas*" whenever you encounter someone and "*adios*" when you part. Inquiring after someone's health or how they passed the night is always appreciated. Avoid using the word "*señorita*" unless you are *sure* the person you are addressing is not married.

When boarding a bus or sitting down in a crowded restaurant it is nice to say "*buenas*" to those around you. This isn't done in the US but, in Panama, people may think you are stuck up if you don't at least smile and acknowledge their presence. In general, people in Panama are quite friendly to strangers. It is normal to strike up a casual conversation with seatmates or others around you. This is good: you can ask questions of the locals you encounter without feeling too nosy.

Panamanians always dress better than Americans do. If you see someone in sweats, shorts or T-shirt, it is almost always a gringo. This does not mean you have to wear a tie at dinner, but it does mean you should attempt to dress a little better than you would at home. Locals just shake their heads at gringos wearing tank tops, halter-tops, shorts and sneakers. Shiny leather shoes and tucked-in shirts are normal for men—dresses or conservative slacks for women. Businessmen may not wear ties, but are sure to be better dressed than their US counterparts.

T-back or thong bathing suits are acceptable at large tourist hotel pools, but going topless is not something that is approved of in Panama. To be comfortable, check out your fellow guests at the pool before appearing in your extremely skimpy bathing outfit. Such bathing suits don't take up much space, so go ahead and pack one, just in case.

Further Reading

- Frederick Kempe. *Divorcing the Dictator*. G.P.Putnam Sons, 1990. ISBN 0-399-13517-0.
- John Dinges. *Our Man in Panama*. Random House, 1990. ISBN 0-394-54910-1.
- Luis G. Carrasquilla. *Trees & Shrubs of Panama*. University of Panama 2005. ISBN 9962-651-08-5.
- Robert S. Ridgely, John A. Gwynne, Jr. *A Guide to the Birds of Panama*. Princeton University Press, 1989. ISBN 0-691-02512-6.
- George R. Angehr, Dodge & Lorna Engleman. *A Bird-Finding Guide to Panama*. Panama Audubon Society, 2007. ISBN 080147423X.
- Eric Bauhaus. *The Panama Cruising Guide*. Eric Bauhaus, 2007. ISBN 9962-00-130-7.
- John Kircher, *A Neotropical Companion*. Princeton University Press, 1999. ISBN 0691009740.
- Kevin Buckley, *Panama: The Whole Story*. Simon and Schuster, 1991. ASIN: B000OTU49E.
- James Howe, *A People Who Would Not Kneel: Panama, the United States, and the San Blas Kuna*. Smithsonian 1998. ISBN 1560988657.
- Sandra Snyder, *Living in Panama*. TanToes S.A. 2007. ISBN 962001560.

Internet Access

Wireless Internet access is now available in almost all hotels in Panama. Unfortunately, the technology is still fairly new, so in many hotels, perhaps most, the connections are poor or unavailable anywhere a little distant from the lobby (like in your room).

Internet cafes abound but you probably won't need to visit one if your hotel has a decent connection.

Language

Spanish is the national language and is spoken without the heavy accents of nearby Venezuela or Cuba. Panamanians tend to cut words short so *pez*, (fish) becomes "*pe'*" and *está* (it is) becomes "*'ta.*"

Due to the long influence of the Americans and their canal, and due to Panama's international importance as a business center, English is widely spoken. Many speak it quite well. I attempt to use my Spanish at all times, even when I know the people I am speaking with speak English better than I speak Spanish. This seems to be appreciated.

Newspapers

There are several dailies published in Panama City. The best, by far, is *La Prensa*, www.prensa.com, a Spanish language daily with a tremendous amount of pages each week devoted to travel and tourism.

The Panama News appears occasionally in English. Their website, www.thepanamanews.com, is worth a visit for opinion, news and tourism information.

Maps

The recently released *National Geographic Panama Adventure Map* is the way to go.

Passport & Visa Regulations

Americans and Canadians are required to have a valid passport and a tourist card. Tourist cards are available at the airport and at airline counters. They entitle you to stay in the country for 30 days. The cards can be extended for an additional 60 days with a little bit of hassle.

Postal Service

The best way to think about postal service in Panama is to realize that they just don't have any. Courier services are the way things move about the country. Official Post Office boxes are almost unobtainable so mailbox centers thrive. Bills are paid in person. Many tourist operations have mail forwarding services based in Miami that forward regular mail by courier.

Telephones

Phones work just about like they do in the US. Be aware that all mobile phones have an extra "6" in front of the number. For instance: 507-6682-5308.

Phone cards are the best way to make overseas calls. You can buy them in small shops and at some hotel front desks. Expect to pay from $0.03 to over $0.25 per minute to the US. Shop around for the best deal.

GSM-based mobile phones work in Panama, although you may have to buy a chip. The best thing to do to stay in touch is simply to buy a cheap local mobile phone from an electronics store or kiosk. There are usually bargains to be had. Many of the more remote parts of the country do not have cell coverage, but I am always surprised when my phone rings while I'm fishing 30 miles out in the Pacific or hiking miles back in a cloud forest.

Time

Panama runs on Eastern Standard Time (GMT–5) and does not adjust for Daylight Savings. Panama is near the equator so the length of day does not vary much. It gets light at about 6am and gets dark about 6pm. It gets dark in a hurry too. There is not much in the way of dusk—it's daytime and all of a sudden it's dark. Plan ahead.

Tipping

In general, Panamanians are not the mad tippers Americans are. It is simply not necessary to tip cab drivers. The fares are almost always an even dollar amount so you don't even need to round up. Most restaurants include a service charge on the bill. Have a look or ask to see if this is so before forking over more dough. I tend to tip bartenders with each drink order, thinking I will get better service for subsequent orders if the bartender knows I'm ready to tip for good service. But don't spoil it for the rest of us.

This is not the US and people just do not tip very much. Except at large, tourist-oriented hotels, no one will be surprised or offended if you keep your change in your pocket.

Tourist Information

IPAT (Instituto Panameño de Turismo) is Panama's tourist agency. Their headquarters are in the Centro Atlapa, Via Israel, Panama City. They also have an office at Tocumen International Airport and in cities around the country. Their role is to help tourists on their way. In reality they offer little more than a few glossy brochures.

Water

Tap water is safe to drink almost everywhere in the country. Bottled water is available all over.

Websites

- **www.panamaaudubon.org** is an excellent resource for birders. They have an interesting list of endemic birds.
- **www.ipat.gob.pa** is the official site for IPAT, Panama's tourist board. The site is nicely designed but has very little actually useful information.
- **www.thepanamanews.com** is an English language newspaper site with news, opinion and travel information.
- **www.tripadvisor.com/ForumHome** is one of the very best sites for itinerary planning. The forums are full of comments from travelers about their experiences in hotels, restaurants, their experiences with tour operators and how their itineraries worked out. Post your questions and you are likely to get useful answers from people who have just come back. A great site.
- **www.canopylodge.com** and **www.canopytower.com** are both nice sites to drop in on from time to time to check out the list of recent sightings in the area. They have masses of links to other informative sites.
- **www.stri.org** is the site for the Smithsonian Tropical Research Institute which maintains extensive research facilities in Panama.

Weights & Measures

Panama, like many countries, is inching over to the metric system. Fuel is still sold by the gallon. Road signs and speed limits are in kilometers.

ESSENTIAL SPANISH

Pleasantries

A simple "*buenas*" works just fine for a casual "hello" or "goodbye" almost anytime of day.

Please – *por favor*
Thank you – *gracias*

You're welcome – *de nada*
Excuse me – *perdóneme, permiso* or *discúlpame*
Good day – *buenos días*
Good night – *buenas noches*
Goodbye – *adiós*
Hello – *hola*
How are you? – *¿Como está Usted?* or *¿Que tal?*
Fine – *muy bien*
Pleased to meet you – *mucho gusto*
Cool, thanks, see you later – *tranquilo*

Everyday Phrases
Yes – *sí*
No – *no*
I don't know. – *No sé.*
Do you speak English? – *¿Habla usted inglés?*
I don't speak Spanish. – *Yo no hablo español*
Friend – *Amigo*
Where? – *¿Donde?*
When? – *¿Cuando?*
Why? – *¿Por que?*
Because – *porque*
How much? – *¿Cuanto?*
How do you say…? – *¿Cómo se dice…?*
Today – *hoy*
Tomorrow – *mañana*
Yesterday – *ayer*
I would like – *quisiera*
Here – *aquí*
There – *allá*
More – *mas*
Less – *menos*
Much – *mucho*
Little – *poco*
Large – *grande*
Small – *pequeño*
Good – *bueno*
Bad – *malo*

Travel Terms

Hotel – *(el) hotel*
Bank – *(el) banco*
Money – *(el) dinero*
Airport – *(el) aeropuerto*
Taxi – *(el) taxi*
Bus – *(el) autobús*
Car – *(el) coche, carro*
Boat – *barco, bota*
Bathroom – *(el) baño*
Gas station – *(la) bomba, gasolinera*
How far is . . . – *¿Que distancia es . . . ?*
Road, highway – *(la) carretera*
Street – *(la) calle*
Avenue – *(la) avenida*

Eating & Drinking

Menu – *menú, lista*
Meat – *(la) carne*
Beef – *(el) bistec*
Pork – *(el) cerdo*
Ham – *(el) jamón*
Chicken – *(el) pollo*
Liver – *(el) hígado*
Fish – *(el) pescado*
Tuna – *atún*
Snapper – *pargo*
Sea bass – *corvina*
Octopus - *pulpo*
Marinated seafood salad – *ceviche*
Seafood – *(los) mariscos*
Shrimp – *(los) camarones*
Cheese – *queso*
Bread - *pan*
Vegetables – *(los) legumbres*
Potato - *papa*
Salad – *ensalada*
Garlic – *ajo*
Raw – *crudo*

Fruits – *(las) frutas*
Pineapple – *(la) piña*
Banana – *(el) plátano, banano*
Orange – *(la) naranja*
Apple – *(la) manzana*
Guava – *(la) guayaba*
Lemon, lime – *limón*
Water – *(el) agua*
Bottled water – *agua mineral*
Milk – *(la) leche*
Coffee – *(el) café*
Black coffee – *café negro, cafe natural*
Coffee with milk – *café con leche*
Tea – *(el) té*
Beer – *(la) cerveza*
Red wine/white wine – *vino tinto / vino blanco*
Glass of water – *(el) vaso de agua*
Glass of wine – *(la) copa de vino*
Soft drink – *(el) refresco*
Smoothie, milkshake – *(el) batido, licuado*
Juice – *(el) jugo*

Panamanian Slang, Localisms & Other Useful Words & Phrases
Swimming place, hot springs – *balneario*
Coffee factory – *beneficio*
Cigarette – *blanco*
Gossip – *bochinche*
Thatched hut, usually a small beachfront restaurant or bar – *bohío*
Gas station – *bomba*
Drunk – *borracho*
Marinated seafood salad – *ceviche*
Corner store – *chinito*
a collective taxi, van or boat – *colectivo*
local bus (red devil) – *diablo rojo*
Wildlife – *fauna silvestre*
Beer – *fría*
Hung over – *goma*
Local cane liquor – *guaro*
Cop car – *hota*

Fried and smashed green plantains – *patacones*
More or less on time – *hora americana*
Marijuana – *mota*
Buck, dollar bill – *palo*
one of the elite, Caucasian upper class – *rabiblanco(a)*
Low status female – *racataca*
Nature trail – *sendero*
You're lookin' good, baby! – *tas buena mami*
Cop – *tongo*
'Bye, take it easy, cool – *tranquilo*
Wealthy show-off – *yeye*

Pronunciation
Spanish is a phonetic language, meaning that words are almost always spelled just as they sound.

Vowels are pronounced roughly as follows:
a – as in *father*
e – as we pronounce a long "a". *Pedro* is pronounced *Paydro* rather than *Peedro*
i – as in *magazine*
o – as in *phone*
u – as in *prune*

There are no silent vowels. For example, *coche* (car) is pronounced KO-chay. A written accent on a vowel means that it is stressed, as in Colón (ko-LONE).

Consonants are pronounced roughly the same as in English, except:
c – like *k* before *a, o* or *u*; like *s* before *e* or *i*
h – always silent
j – like *h* in *home*
ll – like *y* in *yet*
ñ – like *ni* in *union*
z – like *s*

INDEX

Things Change!

Phone numbers, prices, addresses, quality of service – all change. If you come across any new information, we'd appreciate hearing from you. No item is too small! Drop us an e-mail at jopenroad@aol.com, visit us at www.openroadguides.com

PHOTO CREDITS

The following images are from flickr.com: front cover, pp. 52, 136: tanya307; back cover photo and p. 102: Gaira House; pp. 15, 178: Young in Panama; p. 20: Erik Cleves Kristensen; pp. 23, 29, 36, 91, 182: Alexander H.M. Cascone; pp. 3 top, 32, 48, 54, 57 bottom, 128, 151, 155, 172, 173: Lori A. Haskell, Esq.; p. 35: hawkinsa90; pp. 37, 127: Monica&Steve; p. 41: gail548; p. 51: Fabio Bretto; pp. 57 top, 194: Jpeg Jedi; p. 61: Tiago Carneiro Machado; pp. 74, 169: laszlo-photo; p. 102: Gaira House; p. 107: bravenewtraveler; p. 109: CasaLuMa; p. 114: wileypics; p. 118: Mauro Esteban Martinez; p. 128: p. 144: Jeff Bouton/Leica Sport Optics; p. 147: Eric Lin.

The following images are from Bruce Morris: back cover photo and pp. 1, 3 bottom, 8, 9, 10, 17, 43, 44, 49, 50, 60, 62, 64, 65, 67, 69, 70, 80, 83, 106, 119, 121, 129, 138, 140, 150, 166, 168.

The following images are from wikimedia commons: pp. 12, 81: Desi burgos; p. 13: Stan Shebs; pp. 25, 27, 39, 111: DirkvdM; p. 40: Johantheghost: p. 55: Fjdelisle; pp. 85, 98, 101, 159: Mdf; pp. 92, 94: Yves Picq; p. 99: Malene; p. 112; p. 157: Jean-Phillipe Boulet; p. 165: Johantheghost; p. 177: Clearly Ambiguous. *The following images are from istockphoto.com*: Danielho: p. 16; Raclro: p. 19; p. 73: adwalsh. *The following image is from Bridgepix.com*: p. 47. *The following image is from Panama Big Game Fishing*: pp. 72, 96, 142, 170. *The following image is from Marty Casado*: p. 78.